The Men of Warre

The clothes, weapons and accoutrements of the Scots at war 1460-1600

Jenn Scott

For my husband, Sean Chamberlain
Who always sounds as though he actually means it when he says he doesn't mind when I leave piles of research books all over the house.

Helion & Company Limited
Unit 8 Amherst Business Centre
Budbrooke Road
Warwick
CV34 5WE
England
Tel. 01926 499 619
Email: info@helion.co.uk
Website: www.helion.co.uk
Twitter: @helionbooks
Visit our blog http://blog.helion.co.uk/

Published by Helion & Company 2023
Designed and typeset by Mary Woolley, Battlefield Design (www.battlefield-design.co.uk)
Cover designed by Paul Hewitt, Battlefield Design (www.battlefield-design.co.uk)

Text © Jenn Scott 2023
Illustrations © as individually credited
Colour artwork drawn by Seán Ó Brógain © Helion & Company 2023

Every reasonable effort has been made to trace copyright holders and to obtain their permission for the use of copyright material. The author and publisher apologise for any errors or omissions in this work and would be grateful if notified of any corrections that should be incorporated in future reprints or editions of this book.

ISBN 978-1-804510-07-0

British Library Cataloguing-in-Publication Data.
A catalogue record for this book is available from the British Library.

All rights reserved. No part of this publication may be reproduced, stored in a retrieval system, or transmitted, in any form, or by any means, electronic, mechanical, photocopying, recording or otherwise, without the express written consent of Helion & Company Limited.

For details of other military history titles published by Helion & Company Limited contact the above address or visit our website: http://www.helion.co.uk.

We always welcome receiving book proposals from prospective authors.

Contents

Preface		v
1	Introduction	8
2	Bombards, engines, and other instruments of war	14
3	We carried war-raiment and Arms	39
4	Birlinns, ships and galleys	51
5	The Field of Flodden	62
6	The Borders – 'Na, we's all Elliots and Armstrongs'	72
7	Fire and sword	77
8	Uncivil kind of clothes	89
Colour Plate Commentaries		95
Glossary		98
Bibliography		105

Preface

The clothing, weapons and accoutrements of the Scots over a period of one hundred and forty years is obviously quite a wide subject and one that has caused me a few headaches as I have been researching it over the last couple of years, not least because like everyone else I was unable to visit physically any archives or libraries for much of the period of my researches.

This book looks at the clothing, weapons and accoutrements of the Scots at war during the period when Scotland moved from the end of the medieval world to the early modern. In order to establish what the clothing and weapons of the Scots were like during this time. There are three key sources of information: extant garments and weapons, contemporary visual representations, and lastly written materials containing information, descriptions and sometimes prices.

Scotland for most of this period has very few extant clothes and weapons and until the end of the 16th century not many pictures, especially of middling and poorer men. There are however, effigies of elite men dressed in armour from both the Lowlands and the West Coast of Scotland. There are three valuable resources from the Scottish Royal Household:

> The Treasurers' Accounts, which gives information of the clothes and weapons purchased by the Royal Household both for the many men employed by them but also for preparing for war.
> The Exchequer Rolls, are the records of the Comptroller who handled the revenue from crown lands, burghs and customs which was spent on the royal household.
> And from the 16th century, a set of accounts for the Master of Works. The Treasurers' Accounts survive in a fragmentary form from 1473 onwards but are mostly complete from 1488.

The country of Scotland changed a great deal in the time from 1460 to 1600. At the beginning of this period, Scotland was very obviously divided into two quite distinct halves; with the Western seaboard and Isles, dominated by the MacDonald, Lords of the Isles (Rìgh Innse Gall) which culturally and linguistically had much in common with Ireland, and the East and South controlled from Edinburgh by the King of the Scots. Although, it is also true that the recent acquisitions of the Scots crown of Orkney and Shetland had little in common with either since they had until recently been ruled by Norway. However, these cultural dividing lines started to blur a little during the 16th century due to the fall of the Lords of the Isles in 1490 and the Reformation in 1560. Even before then, that the Gaeltacht did not exist in a pure cultural bubble of its own where no hint of the Renaissance touched it or indeed that the makars and sword slippers of Edinburgh were as ignorant of the 'wild Hieland men' as they liked perhaps to pretend. The nobility of the Highlands were by the end of the 16th century Renaissance men as much as the rest of the aristocracy in Scotland, and this is reflected in their clothes, weapons and armour as much as what they read or the way they decorated their houses.

Throughout this book, I will look at what the men who fought in them wore and used in various battles against England, notably Flodden (9 September 1513), the wars of the Rough Wooing (December 1543–March 1551) and Pinkie Cleugh (10 September 1547), as well as some of the clan battles and the Marian civil wars (1568–1573). The 16th century in the Highlands is frequently described as the most turbulent period of its history, a view supported by the name given to it in Gaelic tradition: 'Linn nan Creach' or the 'Age of Forays',[1] although this name is much like the Rough Wooing or the Wars of the Roses in that contemporaries would not have recognised it.[2] The Borders, or the Debatable Lands, were still being shaken loose until the end of the 16th century by regular raids from the Border families. However, there was no equivalent of the Wars of the Roses in Scotland; the Scots crown did not face the kind of repeated significant armed rebellion of its nobility that the English crown experienced during the latter part of the Middle Ages.

Throughout this book I have tried to use contemporary names for clothes, weapons and other items of material culture and language as much as possible except where it would be simply too confusing – you will find a glossary at the end which I hope will help with at least some of the confusion. Although they did not call the parts of armour or indeed clothing as many names as we do and certainly not as many as the Victorians, I have tried to record names as I came across them and in the appropriate languages, which in this case are mostly English, Scots and Gaelic. As ever any mistakes, misspellings or mistranslations are entirely my own fault.

Once again, I am grateful to the Stewart Society for allowing me to use their library; to Elizabeth Quarmby-Lawrence for her sterling work in finding more obscure articles and books, Dr Arran Johnston for discussions on bits of Scottish history during lockdown, Lindsay Webster for heroic scanning of vital articles, my husband, Sean Chamberlain, for buying

---

1 D. Stevenson, *Highland Warrior: Alasdair MacColla and the Civil Wars* (Edinburgh, 1994), p.21.
2 R. M. Crawford, *Warfare in the West Highlands and Isles of Scotland, c. 1544–1615.* (Glasgow, unpublished PhD thesis, 2016) p.13.

PREFACE

books about armour for my birthday, general fact checking, cheering me on and never sighing when I bought yet another book about the Highlands; the rest of my family for their support and patience and, as ever, to my editor, Charles Singleton and also to Stephen Ede-Borrett. I would also like to thank the Dorothy Dunnett Society for their generous support, which allowed me to purchase some of the images in this book.

Edinburgh,
August 2022

1

Introduction

> They spend all their time in wars, and when there is no war they fight each other.[1]

During much of the time covered by this book, Scotland's relationship with its closest neighbour, England, can only be described as turbulent, although there was no major invasion of Scotland by England between 1400 and 1482. Until at least the middle of the 16th century, the shaky peace between the two countries broke down quite frequently into open warfare that required Scotland and its men to be ready to fight. However, the reign of King James II (1437–1460) in the mid 15th century was notable for an ultimately successful series of sieges against the rebellious Black Douglases and their adherents rather than warfare against the auld enemy extensively, which culminated in the forfeiture of his lands and exile of the Earl. Despite this, the King was killed in his attempt to retake Roxburgh Castle in the Borders from the English in 1460. His infant son, James III was knighted with an hundred others after his father died.[2]

Throughout the period, the strong Burgundian influence on the Scots court influenced the clothing worn by the courtiers and the wider elite as well as the increasing importance of chivalry and chivalric display.

Armies in Scotland at this time were still largely put together on the basis of common service and feudal obligations. The feudal levy, which unlike in England, remained a major element of the Scottish army into the 16th century; and, secondly, the common army, in which all men between 16 and 60 years of age and not already serving in a noble retinue, were liable

---

1 P. Hume-Brown (ed.), *Early Travellers in Scotland* (Edinburgh, Nell& Co, 1891), p.43.
2 A. MacDonald, 'The Kingdom of Scotland at War: 1332–1488', in E. Spiers, J. Crang, M. J. Strickland (Eds), *A Military History of Scotland*, (Edinburgh, Edinburgh University Press, 2012, 2014), pp.158–181 at p.173.

INTRODUCTION

to serve. The common army was drilled by royal sheriffs and the officers of the great lords, who held wappenschaws [weapon-showings] at least once a year. At these, the sheriff checked that men owned and maintained suitable equipment for war. Individuals were expected to equip themselves for war according to their position in life.[3] Instructions given to sheriffs in 1513 indicated that gentlemen were expected to muster in plate armour, while common men were to come in jacks and sallets.

The frequency was increased from time to time by Parliament with the addition of troops maintained by money contracts e.g. mercenaries or man rent.[4] For example before the invasion of 1482, Parliament, ordered the frequency of wappenschaws to be raised to once every 15 days.[5] The troops were generally expected to serve at their own expense and mostly bring their own supplies, a factor that limited the ability of Scots armies to take part in a long campaign. Scotland continued to rely on this method of recruitment longer than was the case in England. In 1513, for the Flodden campaign this system was nonetheless successful in producing a large and impressive force.

James III (1460–1488), furnished a number of border castles with artillery and repaired the royal castles of Dunbar and Lochmaben.[6] He followed a policy of peace towards England with the exception of the Anglo–Scottish war of 1480–2. Parliament in 1481 seeing the threat of invasion from England charged the nobility and the bishops to follow suit:

> that hes Castelles neires the Bordures and on the Sea coaste, sik as Sainte Andrewes, Aberdene, Temptallon [Tantallon], Hume, Douglas, Hailis, and especially the Hermitage that is in maist danger, and sik uther Castelles and strengthes, that may be keiped and defended fra our enemies of England. That illk [each] Lord stuff his awin house and strengthen them with victualles, men and artailzierie [fill his house with food, men and guns].[7]

---

3   "Wapynschawin *n.*". *Dictionary of the Scots Language*. 2004. Scottish Language Dictionaries Ltd. Accessed 5 May 2022.
4   A. MacDonald, 'Courage, Fear and the Experience of the Later Medieval Soldier', *The Scottish Historical Review*, volume XCII 2, no. 2235: October 2013, (Edinburgh 2013) pp.179–206. J. W. Armstrong, 'Local Society and the Defence of the English Frontier in Fifteenth Century Scotland: The War Measures of 1482', *Florilegium* 25 (Toronto, University of Toronto, 2008), pp.127–49. Manrent was the undertaking to be someone's ss 'man' or supporter. In return the patron (often but not exclusively a clan chief or chieftain) promised his maintenance and backing to the supporter
5   J. W. Armstrong, 'Local society and the defence of the English frontier in fifteenth century Scotland', p.132.
6   G. Stell, 'Late Medieval Defences in Scotland', D. Caldwell, D (ed.), *Scottish Weapons and Fortifications*, (Edinburgh, John Donald, 1981) p.23.
7   Quoted in G. Stell, 'Late Medieval Defences in Scotland', p.25.

THE MEN OF WARRE

In June 1482, Richard, Duke of Gloucester entered Scotland with the intention of putting the King's brother, Alexander Stewart, Duke of Albany on the throne. However, Richard was unsuccessful despite reaching Edinburgh. At Lauder, in the Borders, James III was seized as he brought together the Scottish army. The King was taken to Edinburgh Castle. The invaders marched to Edinburgh in early August, Albany negotiated a compromise for his return to Scotland, and the English army returned south, capturing Berwick by the end of the month. James III was killed six years later in the aftermath of his defeat at the hands of his son and his supporters at the battle of Sauchieburn in 1488.

Some stability was restored to Scotland under his son, James IV (1488–1513), although his reign was not entirely free of military campaigns. James used artillery to capture small castles like Duchal, in Renfrew as part of his suppression of the Western Rebellion in 1489.[8] Indeed, the King went out in person to lay siege to Duchal and Crookston Castles where it is likely that *Mons Meg* was present.[9] James' reign and love of war, 'he does not think it right to begin any warlike undertaking without being himself first in danger', came to a disastrous conclusion for the Scots at Flodden in 1513.[10] A change in tactics in the use of the Scottish long spears or pikes in favour of new techniques from the Continent at this battle contributed to the death of the King and much of the nobility.[11]

Flodden saw the centuries long struggle with England renewed. Scotland essentially became a battleground fought over by the French and English. Flodden had been fought by the Scots in support of a French alliance, and this policy was furthered during the minority of James V by the Regent Albany (1513–1542). In 1530, King James V acted against the lawless Border clans of the 'Debatable lands' between Scotland and England and imprisoned some of the border lairds for their lack of action. The King also managed to damage the strength of the Armstrongs, by hanging Johnnie Armstrong of Gilnockie and 31 others at Carlanrig Chapel. The Borders however were not actually pacified until the reign of James VI.

James' reign saw the humiliating defeat of the Scots at the hands of the English at Solway Moss in 1542. It was this decade that saw wide adoption of gunpowder weapons by the Scots.[12] 'Gunnis, hagbuttis, handbowis and

---

8   G. Philips, in *Scotland in the Age of Military Revolution*, p.189.
9   T. Dickson, (Ed.); 'Treasurers' Accounts', *Compotathesaurariorum Regum Scotorum*. (H.M. General Register House, Edinburgh, 1877), volume 1, p. ccxxii.
10 Hume-Brown, *Early Travellers in Scotland*, p.41.
11 'The Scots advanced 'in good order, after the Almanynes [German] manner' quoted by G. Philips in 'Scotland in the Age of Military Revolution, 1488–1560', in J. A. Crang, E. M. Spiers & M. J. Strickland (Eds), *A Military History of Scotland*, (Edinburgh, Edinburgh University Press, 2014), pp.182–208 at p.185.
12 G. Philips, *Scotland in the Age of Military Revolution*, p.187. The idea that the Scots were slow to adopt firearms comes from Patten. This is not true as will be seen throughout this book.

vther small artelȝerie now common lievs it in all cuntreis.'¹³ The Scots' defeat at Solway Moss seems to have been a major cause of the death of the King not long afterwards. James' infant daughter, Mary's (1542–1567) accession to the throne at six days old increased the English determination to win their neighbour, firstly by marriage to Henry VIII's heir, the young Prince Edward and secondly by conquest. By 1543, a sea of political and religious change had swept across Europe. Henry VIII had broken with Rome in the decade before and Scotland was under huge pressure as the only Catholic country remaining in Northern Europe. The wars known later as the 'Rough Wooing' commenced. The defeat of the Scots Army at Pinkie Cleugh on 'Black Saturday' in 1547, often called the first modern battle as there was artillery, sea and foot combat, led to the subsequent establishment of English garrisons in Scotland. Eventually, the French intervened on the side of the Scots and they were ultimately the victors.

The Highlands were also in a period of instability, not only were there external pressures from England like the rest of Scotland, but there were also internal pressures. Towards the end of the 15th century, the MacDonald Lordship of the Isles that had dominated the Western seaboard of Scotland and Isles since the twelfth century collapsed due to a mixture of internal disunity and pressure from both James III and James IV. The forfeiture of the Lordship to the Crown took place in 1493. The Western seaboard at this point began its long pull away from Ireland. The people in this area had dressed and fought for centuries in ways that had shown their cultural links with Ireland, including the long history of Galloglass warriors in Ireland, whether as settlers with Scottish heritage or those who would visit as mercenaries for a season or on a raid and return.

Much of what might now be recognised as Highland culture emerged in the period after the fall of the Lordship of the Isles. It had been virtually a kingdom within Scotland, even going so far as to make treaties with England. By the 17th century, the clothing and weapons of the two countries looked different [and indeed the sort of Gaelic that they spoke was also different] however for much of the time of this book the people of the Western Highlands looked much like many of the people in Ireland – there were of course some important differences. The men and women around Inverness and on the east were different again.¹⁴ With the disappearance of the Lordship of the Isles there was no effective regional authority to settle disputes; Edinburgh and royal authority was often simply too remote to be successful in this role. Additionally, as in the Borders raids were a way of proving masculinity and identity:

---

13 "Artilȝerie *n.*". *Dictionary of the Scots Language*. 2004. Scottish Language Dictionaries Ltd. Accessed 6 May 2021. Specifically APS, ii 371, c.11. This act of Parliament was written in 1540.

14 The Orkneys only became Scottish in the 15th century, thus they were also different and very definitely not Highland or even particularly Scottish.

> Every Heir, or young Chieftain of a Tribe, was oblig'd in Honour to give a publick Specimen of his Valour, before he was own'd and declar'd Governor or Leader of his people, who obey'd and follow'd him upon all Occasions. This Chieftain was usually attended with a retinue of young Men of Quality, who had not beforehand given any Proof of their Valour, and were ambitious of such an Opportunity to signalize themselves. It was usual for the Captain to lead them, to make a desperate Incursion upon some Neighbour or other that they were in Feud with; and they were oblig'd to bring by open force the Cattel they found in the Lands they attack'd, or to die in the Attempt. After the Performance of this Achievement, the young Chieftain was ever after reputed valiant and worthy of Government, and such as were of his Retinue acquir'd the like Reputation. This Custom being reciprocally us'd among them, was not reputed Robbery, for the Damage which one Tribe sustain'd by this Essay of the Chieftain of another, was repair'd when their Chieftain came in his turn to make his Specimen.[15]

The first half of the 16th century saw the MacDonalds and their allies struggle against Royal authority in an attempt to restore the Lordship of the Isles. It is possible to identify seven serious rebellions in this period, all of which attempted to restore the MacDonalds in some form, a clear indication of the strong resistance felt towards the crown's measures. In 1506, for example, when there was an attempt at rebellion and putting Torcail McLeod of Lewis's nephew Donald Dubh into the Lordship of the Isles,[16] James commanded a fleet up to the Isles to stop the rebellion and display his strength.

The King had hugely increased his expenditure on ships at this time, building the great ship *Margaret*, named after his wife, as well as improving his capacity to build ships at New Haven in Edinburgh.

The Earl of Huntly led the force against Lewis with a contingent of ships, including the *Raven* that, with its cannon, helped reduce Stornoway Castle in 1506. The last rebellion occurred in 1545, a few years after James V had annexed the lordship to the crown during his expedition to the Isles in 1540.[17] Those in authority complained frequently at what they saw as the lawless nature of the 'wild Highlands and their people' while at the same time exploiting feuds between clans and clan leaders when it was convenient. In 1543, Regent Arran released the imprisoned Clanranald

---

15 M. A Martin, *Description of the Western Islands of Scotland*, (Edinburgh, The Mercat Press, 1982), p.167. *Miscellany of the Maitland Club, Consisting of Original Papers and Other Documents Illustrative of the History and Literature of Scotland*, (Maitland, Glasgow, 1840–47) pp.101–2.

16 Forfeiture of 'Torcule Makloid of the Lewis', 24 December 1505. APS ii, pp.263–4.

17 A. Cathcart, 'The Forgotten '45: Donald Dubh's Rebellion in Archipelagic Context'. *The Scottish Historical Review*, volume 91, no. 232, 2012, p.239.

chief along with other 'Irish' to divert the attention of Argyll and Huntly, who were supporters of his main rival, Cardinal Beaton. As a consequence, Clanranald fought the Frasers in one of the largest clan battles of the 16th century in the following summer.[18] Clan battles continued into the reign of James VI, with these too adapting to the changing technologies so that the gun and the pistol gradually became more important than the axe or bow on the field. Highlanders were present at the siege of Roxburgh in 1460, in James IV's campaign in the north of England in 1490s, Flodden in 1513 and Pinkie Cleugh in 1547. The Earl of Argyll's forces and the numbers of men he could command were a vital part of all of these campaigns.

The Scots, unlike many other countries in Northern Europe, believed for the most part that men rather than fortifications or mercenaries were the most effective way to defend their country.[19] Nonetheless, border towns like Roxburgh and Peebles had walls by the latter part of the 16th century.[20] Haddington and Leith were both fortified extensively during long sieges in the new *Trace Italienne* style although little evidence of either of these remain visible, and other border strongholds and potentially vulnerable castles in the Highlands were reinforced at various points during the period covered by this book.[21] Mercenaries [wageours] were something that Scottish governments rarely paid for, thus they were not a significant part of any Scots army. When they did appear it was mostly only in small numbers, as in 1455 when Parliament agreed to a force of twelve hundred spearmen and archers, divided into three groups, to guard the border with England, and again in 1482; or the insignificant numbers in 1497, 'Giffin to Henry Fowlis to the wageours that lay in Coldinghame.'[22] James IV did employ 60 landsknechts in 1495,[23] but that again this was small scale despite their swagger and colour.

---

18 This was, of course, 'the Battle of the Shirts' [Blàr na Léine].
19 D. Caldwell, 'The Defence of the Scottish Border', *Journal of the Sydney Society for Scottish History*, volume 12, (Sydney 2010), p.59.
20 D. Caldwell, 'The Defence of the Scottish Border', *Journal of the Sydney Society for Scottish History*, volume 12, (Sydney 2010), p.66
21 Haddington was fortified by the English and Leith by the French, so they possibly don't count. See J. Cooper, 'What's missing here? Homing in on Haddington's lost defences', *Journal of Conflict Archaeology*, volume 5, no. 1, 2009, pp.141–62. "artalzere of Donglas [was taken] to Dumbar, and pyonarres with pikis, spadis and schulis to caste doun the fort and strenth of Donglas', and the 'artalzere of the fort of Lauder [was taken] to the castell of Hume witht pikis, schulis and mattokis to caste doun the fort', 1550 TA IX, 421; see also. 423–424.
22 1497 TA I 346.
23 G. Phillips, 'In the Shadow of Flodden: Tactics, Technology and Scottish Military Effectiveness, 1513–1550', *The Scottish Historical Review*, vol. 77, no. 204, 1998, pp.162–182 at p.165.

2

Bombards, engines, and other instruments of war

> Here by great misfortune, his worthie prince Iames the second, was slaine by the slice of a great peece of artillerie, which by ouercharging chanced to breake[1]

King James II died in the attempt to capture Roxburgh Castle, which had been an English outpost in the Southern Uplands of the Borders for at least a century. His father, James I had failed to retake it 24 years earlier. It was during this unsuccessful siege that there had been one of the most significant early uses of guns by the Scottish army; the King had ordered the purchase of bombards and *'aliis instrumentis et apparatibus bellicis'* [other instruments and equipment for war], and hired gunners and artillery workers from Germany.[2] His son however was not killed as a result of hostile gunfire from the English defenders of Roxburgh in 1460, instead it was a fragment of his own bombard, probably but not definitely a gun called *The Lion*, which burst under the strain of firing.[3] *The Lion* unfortunately disappeared from the sources after the siege although it is possible that it accompanied the Scottish forces that campaigned with the Lancastrians in 1461. Roxburgh was actually a Scottish victory despite the King's death and the Scots army moved across the border and successfully attacked Wark in Northumberland.[4] The famous bombard *Mons Meg* was also at the

---

1 R. Holinshed, *Holinshed's Chronicles of England, Scotland and Ireland, volume 5*, (London: J. Johnson, 1807–08), p.13.
2 M. French, https://flemish.wp.st-andrews.ac.uk/2015/11/06/guns-and-gunpowder-in-late-medieval-scotland-influences-from-flanders [accessed 1 April 2021].
3 There is a mention of payments made for damage to *The Lion* when it was put on board ship. TA 1, p. ccxxi.
4 A. Hodge, *Edinburgh Castle: The Medieval Documents* (Edinburgh, Historic

BOMBARDS, ENGINES, AND OTHER INSTRUMENTS OF WAR

siege.[5] *The Lion* had been brought from Flanders in 1430 by his father. The contemporary chronicler, Walter Bower, said that it had this on it:

> For the illustrious James, worthy prince of the Scots.
> Magnificent king, when I sound off, I reduce castles.
> I was made at his order; therefore I am called 'Lion.'[6]

In the words of the 16th century Scottish chronicler, Robert Lindsay of Pitscottie, the arrival of Scottish reinforcements:

> made the king so blyth that he commandit to charge all the gunes, and give the castle ane new volie. But quhill this prince, more curious nor became the majestie of ane king, did stand near hand by, quhair the artylliarie wer discharirged, his thigh bone was dung in tuo be ane piece of anemis framed gune, that brak in the schutting: be the quhilk he was strukin to the ground, and died hastily thairefter.[7]

The Scots were certainly using guns by the 1380s and possibly earlier, but mostly with expert Flemish gunners.[8] Flanders was the established centre of gunpowder technology at this time and all over Europe royal households employed gunners from there for their expertise.[9] The Artillery is recorded as a separate department within the Royal Household in 1436, and that is also from when a record of the first pay for a Master Gunner survives.[10] *The Lion* was the first heavy gun suitable for use in sieges in Scotland. On campaign in the 1450s it travelled in convoy; one cart for the bombard, one for the gunstones, one for the army's supply of arrows and so on.[11] A bronze bombard, made along with other 'bombards, engines and other instruments of war'.[12]

    Scotland, 2018), p.493.
5 *Mons* was so heavy that even a team of oxen couldn't move her more than three miles (five kilometres) a day.
6 K. Stevenson, *Power and Propaganda: Scotland 1306–1488*, (Edinburgh, Edinburgh University Press, 2014) p.187.
7 R. Lindsay, *The Chronicles of Scotland*, 2 volumes (Edinburgh: G. Ramsay and Company, 1814), volume I, p.159.
8 D. H. Caldwell, ' Royal Patronage of Arms and Armour', p. 74. There is some earlier evidence of artillery in Scotland in Jean Froissart's account of Scots using cannon against Stirling Castle in 1341. *Froissart's Chronicles*, John Jolliffe, ed. and trans. (London, 2001), p.115.
9 K. Stevenson, *Power and Propaganda…* p.187. A. Hodge, *Edinburgh Castle: The Medieval Documents* (Edinburgh, Historic Scotland, 2018), p.489.
10 A. Hodge, *Edinburgh Castle: The Medieval Documents*, p.31.
11 K. Stevenson, *Power and Propaganda* p.187.
12 K. Stevenson, *Power and Propaganda* p.488.

THE MEN OF WARRE

Mons Meg at Edinburgh Castle. In the fifteenth century, Mons needed to be winched on to a cart. (©Sean Chamberlain)

Bombards were key symbols of royal power as they were costly to manufacture, difficult to move around and dangerous to use. Owning and using them showed that James was a member of a small, elite club of European princes who could afford to wage war with prestige items like these in terms of resources and manpower. However Scotland certainly needed effective artillery to be able retain its sovereignty against a well-armed and increasingly powerful England. Additionally, in the 1450s, against the defiance of the belligerent Douglases, who had managed to acquire their own powerful artillery and as such threw out a challenge to the power and authority of the Stewart kings. Fortunately, Scotland's good relationship with Burgundy, cemented by a marriage between James II and the Duke of Burgundy's niece – Mary of Gueldres – in 1450, helped to ensure Scotland's supply of weaponry.

The big gun of Threave, *Messenger*, was brought to Edinburgh in 1455 after their defeat. There was also a smaller gun called *Tabard* that came to Scotland with *Mons Meg* in 1457.[13] A further six serpentines were brought to Edinburgh from Threave in 1473. *Mons Meg*, and another cannon later called *Duchal*, were at the siege of Dumbarton in 1489.[14] By the end of the century there may have been as many as 30 guns at the Castle. These were breech-loading iron guns such as the falcons, 'To the pynouris that brocht the falcoun gunnis furth of the Castell to pas to Leith'[15]

---

13 A. Hodge, *Edinburgh Castle: The Medieval Documents*, p.31. NB, Mons Meg wasn't actually called 'Mons Meg' until at least the 17th century.
14 1489 TA 123,4.
15 1505 TA III 141.

BOMBARDS, ENGINES, AND OTHER INSTRUMENTS OF WAR

In the years before the siege of Roxburgh, the custumars [collectors of customs] of Edinburgh and Linlithgow spent a great deal of money on artillery. The custumars of Linlithgow bought military engines [*instrumentis*], carriages (for the guns), iron, timber, barrels, and other items for the siege and the destruction of Abercorn – which was altogether razed to the ground – as well as the tower of Inveravon during the five years before Roxburgh, where James sought to end the rebellion of Earl Douglas.[16] The Douglas stronghold of Threave Castle in Galloway is thought to have had the earliest known artillery work in Scotland, which comprised a curtain wall around an imposing tower house with a continuous external batter to protect it against cannon fire. The garrison only eventually surrendered after bribery.[17] Despite this James' bombards played an important part in crushing Douglas.[18] In a sad foreshadowing of James' own death, his French gunner Alan Pantour died during the siege when one of his own guns exploded. There was also legislation in 1455 and again in 1471, which obliged the nobility, 'Certane of the gret baronys were asked to provide 'cartis of weir', bishops and burghs to provide themselves with 'carts of war' (carts mounted with field guns) for protection of the realm, however it would appear that not many of them actually did so.[19]

The law of 1455 stated:

> should our old enemies [the English] happen to invade the realm it would be expedient to cause certain carts of war for the defence of the realm to be made by prelates [and] barons according to the faculty and power of the persons, the lords think it expedient that the said carts of war be made by the said persons as for this time.[20]

It is evident though from this and other conflicts that nobles and lairds did actually have guns. Later Acts of Parliament of 1535 and of 1540 required them to also have 'hagbuts of crok' (small pieces of artillery fitted with a mounting hook).[21] There were plenty of gun makers to be found throughout the Lowlands and the Northeast of Scotland by the latter part of the 16th century, but records for the Highlands are unfortunately much more

---

16   G. Burnett, J. Stuart et al (Eds), *Rotuli Scaccarii Regum Scotorum. The Exchequer Rolls of Scotland*, (Edinburgh, H.M. General Register House, 1878–1908), volume 6, p.31.
17   C. Tabraham, 'The Scottish Medieval Towerhouse as Lordly Residence in the Light of Recent Excavations', (PSAS 118 1988), p.271. 'Late Medieval Defences in Scotland', in Caldwell (ed.), *Scottish Weapons and Fortifications*, p.47.
18   D. H. Caldwell, 'Royal Patronage of Arms and Armour', pp.74–75. K. Stevenson, *Power and Propaganda*, p.45.
19   *RPS*, A1474/5/5. Date accessed: 16 May 2021.TA, volume 1, p ccxxi
20   *RPS*, 1471/5/5. Date accessed: 5 May 2021
21   There are two extant examples in the National Museum of Scotland, another in the collection of Glasgow Museums and six others in private collections.

difficult to trace, although there is some evidence of lairds in the Highlands buying guns by the mid 16th century.

> Euery landit man … sall haue ane hagbute of found [made of cast metal] callit hagbute of crochert with thar cawmys, [mould for bullets] bullettis and pellokis off leid or irne [cannonball of lead or iron].[22]

These do not seem to have been taken on royal expeditions or to wappenschaws, where men met and demonstrated that they had weapons appropriate to their station.[23] The Scots army was composed at least in theory of all the men between the ages of 16 and 60 – who were to turn out 'weill bodin in fear of weir'.[24] And that 'our lords lieges should not be bereft of harness when it is needed, and that football and golf be discontinued in the future, and butts made up and shot used.'[25] For artillery, especially the great bombards, to get to battles or sieges it took many men, horses, and oxen. In 1497, when James IV besieged Norham Castle the guns required 187 horses, 110 drivers, 221 men with spades and mattocks, 61 quarrymen and masons, and 12 carpenters to accompany the culverins and smaller guns, as well as the actual gunners.[26]

The earliest evidence for gun casting in Scotland is in the early 1470s when it was being carried out at, or near, the Blackfriars in Edinburgh.[27] In 1473/4 James III paid William Goldsymth to make a mould, 'Wil Goldmyth that makis the gun'.[28] However, it was Ranald, a Frenchman, who made another mould in April 1474.[29] In 1496, money was paid 'to the man who castis the chameris to the brass gun'.[30] Quarrymen were hired to make the gunstones. 'Iohne, quareour, for correkking of gunstanis [to make the gun stones right]'.[31] In addition to his other guns and artillery, the 'great bombard' *Mons Meg* was given to James II by Philip the Good, Duke of Burgundy on his marriage to Mary of Gueldres at Holyrood Palace in 1449.[32] For a

---

22 "Pellok n.". *Dictionary of the Scots Language*. 2004. Scottish Language Dictionaries Ltd. Accessed 5 May 2021 <http://www.dsl.ac.uk/entry/dost/pellok_n_2
23 Caldwell, D., 'Royal Patronage of Arms and Armour', pp.74–75. *RPS*, 1471/5/5. Date accessed: 5 May 2021. "Wapynschawin n.". *Dictionary of the Scots Language*. 2004. Scottish Language Dictionaries Ltd. Accessed 5 May 2022
24 D. H. Caldwell, 'Royal Patronage of Arms and Armour', p.73.
25 *RPS*, 1471/5/6. Date accessed: 16 May 2022.
26 TA, 1pclv
27 D. Caldwell, *Edinburgh Castle's Role as a Gun House*, (Edinburgh, Historic Environment Scotland, 2018), p.2.
28 TA 1 49.
29 TA, 1, p. ccxvii, p.47.
30 1496, TA 1, 294
31 1496 TA 1 295.
32 K. Stevenson, 'Power and Propaganda', p.44. Although he actually didn't receive it until seven years later, in 1457.

BOMBARDS, ENGINES, AND OTHER INSTRUMENTS OF WAR

long time *Mons Meg* was believed to have been one of the biggest guns of her type in the world, although the great bronze Dardanelles Gun of the Ottomans made in 1464 was probably comparable in size. *Mons Meg*, however, unlike the Dardanelles Gun, or *Faule Mette* from Burgundy, was practically useful to the Scots for a long period.

Like other royalty, James II also hired experienced gunners from the Continent. Two years before the siege at Roxburgh in 1458, a master of artillery, William Bonar of Rosay had been appointed.[33] Guns and munitions were kept at Linlithgow Palace as well as Edinburgh Castle in the reign of James II and there was a gun house (*domus bumbardie*) in Stirling Castle, which was first recorded in 1475.[34]

In 1460, the guns at Edinburgh Castle had repairs done on the windlass for the bombards, (*de le wyndspakis bumbardi*).[35] This is because the guns did not yet have wheeled carriages but instead would travel in carts and then fire from tables, so they needed to be winched into the carts and winched back out. Some time before the death of James III in 1488, he was given some new bronze guns from the French.[36] These cast bronze guns were much more robust than his earlier wrought iron pieces. Additionally they were cast with trunnions (supporting cylindrical projections, on both sides of the barrel to make it simpler to mount onto the carriages for transport and firing).[37]

However for the majority of time that a Scottish royal gun foundry was in existence, it was in Edinburgh Castle, the royal guns were kept there, too, apart from artillery on active service or employed to defend other royal fortresses. James I and II certainly employed specialists to look after their guns, although an actual core of regular gunners, based in Edinburgh Castle, probably only became a fixed item of the Royal Household in the reign of James IV, or just possibly in the time of his father, James III. Sadly the records which listed the amounts paid, the appointments of gunners, and give details of their spending do not survive in any significant quantity until the 16th century,[38] although there are glimpses, such as 'Dietrich Gunner' cleaning the King's bombards (*purgatione*).[39]

In 1473 six small serpentines were moved with powder (*parvorum bumbardorum dictorum serpentynis cum pulveris*) in two carriages with four horses (*curribus*) from Threave to Edinburgh Castle.[40] In 1488, *Mons*

---

33 D. H. Caldwell, 'Royal Patronage of Arms and Armour', p.74. The next one known is Allan, Lord Cathcart in 1482/3
34 *ER* vii: 275
35 It cost £10 Scots, 18s 10d ER vii. 294 5.
36 Caldwell, 'Royal Patronage of Arms and Armour', p.75.
37 D. H. Caldwell, 'How Well Prepared was James IV to Fight by Land and Sea in 1513?' *Journal of the Sydney Society for Scottish History 14*, 2013 (Sydney, 2013), pp.33–75.
38 D. H. Caldwell, *Edinburgh's Gun House*, p.21.
39 ER vii. 422.
40 ER iv 163.

Meg was moved out of Edinburgh Castle for the siege of Dumbarton. '£8 8s; drinksilver for the gunners when they cartit Mons.'[41] When the King was besieging the castles of Duchal and Crookston, the guns were transported drawn by oxen, the responsibility of supplying them was the duty of the sheriffs of the sheriffdoms through which the guns passed.[42] 'To James of Douglas the comptroller be commande by the King and Lordis to mak provision again the Kingis passing to Duchale.' The King had quarrymen move the culverins from Stirling for the siege of Dumbarton that year also. Culverins were a form of muzzle-loading handgun that fired iron shot. 'To Qwariour … to pas to Stirling to get culuerinis to bring to the felde.'[43] In 1501, April: Fifty-four ells of Breton canvas (Bertane cammes) to be cloths to dry the gunpowder on in the castle, and to be two bags (pokis) to bear it forth. This is likely to be an early reference to the mix of gunpowder called 'culverin powder' made by soaking the chemicals in whisky[44].

On 13 September 1496, the Scots artillery left Restalrig, which was then near Edinburgh, they went south via Haddington in East Lothian and then over the Lammermuir Hills, crossed the Tweed, about 80 miles away (approximately 129 kilometres), 8 days later on 21 September. Even this progress was only made possible by the decision to hire horses rather than oxen.[45] 143 carters with their carts, and 196 horses were paid to carry the guns, their equipment, the tents and other items. 20 gentlemen also rode with the carts. 'xx gentilmen that raid with artailzery.'[46]

The ordnance at Edinburgh Castle in 1496 was two great curtalds (short cannon) sent from France, 'ten falcons/little serpentines; thirty cart guns with chambers; sixteen closed carts with spears, stones, powders, and other materials for guns'.[47] The year after, the Master of Artillery, Sir Robert Ker hired 100 workmen, five smiths and carpenters to 'pas with Mons'.[48] He also deployed eight oxen 'to draw the artillery', slower than horses they took perhaps two weeks to pull the heavy guns over the hills to the south.[49] Caldwell estimates that it would take 17 horses or 36 oxen to pull a cannon.[50] Oxen were slower but more readily available as they pulled ploughs and therefore could be commandeered for royal service rather than having to be hired. There are still nine eighteen inch (457mm) stone balls at Norham Castle, which were probably fired by *Mons Meg*.[51]

---

41 1488 TA I 115.
42 1489 TA I 112,3, 4.
43 TA I 122, Caldwell, Edinburgh's Gun House, p.38.
44 1501 TA II 24. Hodge, A, *Edinburgh Castle: The Medieval Documents*, p.159.
45 1496 TA, I 280, 291, 295, 297, 300.
46 1496 TA 1 300
47 Conway, A., *Henry VII's Relations with Scotland and Ireland 1485-98*, (Cambridge, CUP, 1932), p108
48 1497 TA, I 346-7, 349.
49 1497 TA, I 346-7, 346.
50 Caldwell, D. 'Edinburgh Castle's Role as a Gun House', p.37.
51 Caldwell, D. H., 'How Well Prepared was James IV to Fight by Land and Sea', p.50.

BOMBARDS, ENGINES, AND OTHER INSTRUMENTS OF WAR

In the early 15th century there were several thousand Scots troops in French service, probably reaching a peak between 1419 and 1424 at about 15,000 men. The twenty-four Scottish archers of the French *Garde de la Manche* were the most famous example. They were most likely organised to protect the Dauphin in 1419. The bodyguard of the Duke of Burgundy was also a corps of twenty-four archers: first documented in 1420, it can however probably be traced back to the unit of Highland archers recruited by John the Fearless, Duke of Burgundy(1404–1419) in 1411. The Duke of Orleans had also a bodyguard of Scottish archers in 1412, although they presumably ceased to exist as a unit at Agincourt in 1415.[52] The medieval Scots kings had a guard of archers, although it is difficult find reliable references to them in the records.[53] There is a description of the Captain's banner of the Scots Guard that may have been carried at the battle of Bosworth in 1485, 'it was of three colours, red, white, and green, and measured six feet in length. Upon its silken folds were emblazoned a golden sun and a figure of St. Michael.'[54]

A medieval stone statue of an angel in the High Kirk of St Giles has what may be the oldest known Arms of Edinburgh, with the castle on the rock shown clearly. Saints' banners – Saint Margaret, Saint Andrew, Saint Duthac, and Saint Columba – as well as the red lion rampant of the Royal Standard of Scotland – were carried in the field by the royal army. The Royal standard was important on the field; in 1426 two clans joined the royal side when it was revealed.[55] In 1488 tartar (silk) was ordered for the King's banner, 'For v quartaris of tartar to the Kingis banere.'[56] Silk was also used to make a red and blue banner for Perkin Warbeck as the Duke of York in 1496.[57]

The lion and unicorn were often used as livery badges and probably on livery collars also.[58] In the reign of James III the use of the unicorn as a royal symbol became more popular. He introduced the unicorn coin and in the 1470s gave at least one livery collar with a unicorn on it.[59] James III knighted Anslem Adornnes from Bruges in 1469 and gave him a livery collar with a unicorn on it.[60] In 1541/2, Andrew Mansion, a carver, was

---

52 Hodge, *Edinburgh Castle: The Medieval Documents,* p.19.
53 Hodge, *Edinburgh Castle: The Medieval Documents*, note on p.538.
54 This is a description of the Captain's standard at Troyes in 1486 from a contemporary description in Davenport Adams, W. H, *Under Many Flags or Stories of Scots Adventurers*, (London, Frederick Warne & Co, 1896), p.30. I am indebted to Ian Brandt for pointing this description out to me.
55 Bower, *Scotichronicon*, volume 8. Pp. 262–3.
56 1489 TA i 163.
57 1496 TA I 293 'double rede taffety..(and)singil blew taffety
58 Stevenson, K, *Power and Propaganda*, p.40. The use of the unicorn was introduced by James I.
59 Stevenson, K, *Power and Propaganda*, p.188
60 Stevenson, K 'The Unicorn, St Andrew and the Thistle: Was There an Order of Chivalry in Late Medieval Scotland?' *The Scottish Historical Review*, vol. 83, no. 215, (Edinburgh, Edinburgh University Press,2004), pp.7–8.

paid for carving the Royal Arms with unicorns, thistles and fleurs-de-lis on a double culverin.[61] It seems most likely that Scots fighting in the Royal army would have had the lion rampant as a badge if they wore anything. The Trinity Altar piece commissioned by Edward Bonkil, Provost of the Collegiate Chapel of the Holy Trinity in Edinburgh in 1473 shows James III's coat of Arms with a lion rampant. The saltire does not seem to have been used on flags or badges until the 16th century. It was James V who popularised the thistle as a royal symbol and was depicted on more than one occasion wearing a livery collar with thistles on it. Although undoubtedly wearing a livery or identifying badge from their lord and marching under a guild, town or saint's banner helped to give a common identity and create a sense of purpose for the inexperienced and generally fairly poorly armed men who provided the bulk of the Scots armies in this period.[62]

Many of the Scots in French service were archers which makes the lack of archers in the royal army all the more baffling. James I passed legislation in 1424 to encourage archery. Further legislation of 1476 stated that 'every man must shoot at least six arrows a week at the butts and if he did not then he would be fined and the money used to buy drinks for the other men.'[63] However despite even this incentive most Scots soldiers fought with spears, swords and axes, although there were bowyers and arrow makers working in all the major east coast cities and towns at this time. The king also bought bowstrings, bolts and crossbows.[64]

In 1438, the Captain at Edinburgh Castle had 19 sheaves of arrows delivered to him, 'For 19 sheathes of arrows made at Dundee and delivered in Edinburgh Castle to the captain of the same, 31s 8d.'[65] 'Bertholomo bowar for arrowis to the Kingis at the buttis.'[66] The majority of archers in any Scots army were Highlanders and much of the money that was spent in the Treasurers' Accounts and elsewhere with bowyers was in fact those making spears rather than bows. 'In 1445, John Boware made bows [*pro arcubus*] at the order of the captain [*ab eodem de mandato captainei*].'[67] Towns and garrisons had crossbows for defence and in the 16th century when gun makers became more common in Scotland they were often called into maintain or make items for them. In 1491, the King sent for 'Bwte

---

61 1541/2 TA VIII 121.
62 R. Jones, *Bloody Banners: Martial Discipline on the Medieval Battlefield* (Woodbridge, S Boydell & Brewer, 2010), p.64.
63 G. Phillips, G. 'In the Shadow of Flodden: Tactics, Technology and Scottish Military Effectiveness, 1513–1550', *The Scottish Historical Review*, volume 77, no. 204, 1998, pp.162–182 at p.166.
64 1511 TA IV 327
65 G. Burnett, J. Stuart, et al (Eds), *Rotuli Scaccarii Regum Scotorum. The Exchequer Rolls of Scotland*, Volume V (Edinburgh, H.M. General Register House, 1878–1908) p60. A sheaf of arrows was considered to be 24 arrows.
66 1487 TA I 337. This particular bowyer was working in Edinburgh.
67 ER v 180.

purcyfant, to pas to Leytht for corsbowis and culueringis'[68] However at the end of the 15th century and the beginning of the 16th century bowyers also did this. 'Strings at the kings command windis cordis and graithing [making] of them.'[69]

An act of Parliament passed on 6 May 1471 which forbade merchants from importing spears or pikes of less than six ells length (approximately five and half metres) and also banned bowyers from making them.[70] Merchants were importing spear and pike shaft lengths as Scotland had little suitable wood left in her forests. This also makes it clear that the Scots were already using spears that were pike length so the tragedy of Flodden was not about using unfamiliar weapons. Hence why many of the spear and axe makers came to be based around Leith as it was Edinburgh's port and presumably why one of the many variations on the axe was known as a Leith axe.

> That na merchandis bryng speris in this realme … bot gif thai conten sex eln and of a clyft na at na bowar within the realme mak ony speris bot gif thai conten the samyn lentht'

The same act stipulated that yeomen who could not handle a bow should have a:

> good axe and a targe of leather to resist the shot of England.[71]

Then 10 years later, the law stated that:

> every axeman who has neither spear nor bow shall have a wooden or leather targe according to the fashion of the example that shall be sent to each sheriff.'[72]

This does imply that not every Scots man was providing himself with a targe, whether made of wood or leather, however certainly some of them were. John Boware also made spears or lances [*pro lanceis*] for the lord King's use [*usus domini regus*].[73] Thomas Boware, made spears and a 'ledin mellis' [a lead mace] in 1473.[74] In 1481 the act was amended to, no spears other than

---

68 1491 TA I 181.
69 1506–7 TA. III 375. William Macom was working in Edinburgh.
70 *RPS* 1471/4/5. Date accessed: 27 April 2021.
71 *RPS*, 1471/5/6. Date accessed: 15 May 2022.
72 *RPS*, 1481/4/6. Date accessed: 16 July 2021.
73 ER v 181.
74 TA I. 66.

those of five and half ells in length or five ells before the burr [the barb of the spear].

> That thar be na speris made in tyme to cum nor sald that is schortar than five elne & a half or velne at the leist before the bur & of gretnes according tharto.[75]

In 1488, James III at Sauchieburn according to Pitscottie had 1,000 gentlemen 'well horsed' wearing jacks and carrying spears. George Buchanan, also writing his *History* in the latter part of 16th century claimed that the success of the rebel main battle ostensibly led by the future James IV was largely down to the greater length of the rebels' spears over those of the King's men.[76] This was to have an effect on future battles.

Spears were divided into those that were for war and peace for example jousting lances and war spears. In 1496, John Main a bowyer from Edinburgh supplied 20 'speris to the raid of Hume' and' 30 'jousting speris'.[77] A few years later in 1502, he was making 'thre rede [red] speris' for banners or pennants and 'thre quhit' [white] speris.[78] They were also making *broggit* staves, which had a heavy iron head from which spikes projected in all directions, sometimes with a spearhead attached as well. The king levied for his expedition into England in 1496 a tax that was referred to, as the tax of spears or spear silver.[79] Sir John Ramsay, in a letter to Henry VII from Berwick on 8 September 1496 said he saw at Edinburgh Castle sixteen carts for spears[80].

The only significant piece of medieval plate armour still in existence from Scotland is the crown plate of a helm, which is now in the collections of Glasgow Museums.[81] As Dr Caldwell has pointed out: 'the evidence for the armour worn in Scotland in the 15th and 16th centuries comes almost entirely from funeral monuments and documentary sources.'[82] For example, Laurance, an armourer who had first arrived in Scotland in the train of Perkin Warbeck in 1495, was paid in 1502, 'for the dichting [putting into good order] of the Kingis harnes'.[83] Some of the finest secular effigies in the

---

75 Item, it is ordained that in the future no spears are to be made or sold which are shorter than five ells and a half or five ells at the least before the bur. *RPS* 1481/4/5. Date accessed: 27 April 2021.
76 Caldwell, D H 'How Well Prepared was James IV to Fight by Land and Sea in 1513?', *Journal of the Sydney Society for Scottish History 14*, 2013, pp.38–39.
77 1496 TA 1 310
78 1502 TA II 348, 363. D. H. Caldwell, 'Royal Patronage of Arms and Armour', p.86.
79 1496 TA I 312, 324.
80 1496 TA, I, 280, 291, 295.
81 T. E. Capwell, 'Observations on the Armour Depicted on Three Mid–15th Century Military Effigies in the Kirk of St. Nicholas, Aberdeen, *Journal of the Armour Research Society*, 1, 2005, p.5.
82 D. H. Caldwell, 'Royal Patronage of Arms and Armour', p.75.
83 1502 TA II 351.

BOMBARDS, ENGINES, AND OTHER INSTRUMENTS OF WAR

Lowlands are from wealthy Scottish families that were keen to emphasise their often relatively newly acquired knightly status.[84] The Forrester family whose splendid effigies are in Corstorphine Old Parish Church in Edinburgh were a good example of this kind of successful late medieval social climbing.[85] The Lowland effigies, of which there are 80 extant, and of those 35 depict men in full plate armour much like in England, the Low Countries and France unlike the West coast Highland effigies, which have considerable stylistic differences, as well as mostly depicting men in light armour.[86]

Sir John's body, decapitated by Cromwell's soldiers in 1650, is clad in plate armour, and his wife is shown wearing an elaborate gown. The effigies bear traces of black and red paint, part of the original decoration of the tomb and his heraldic colours, Corstorphine Old Parish Church, Edinburgh. (© RCAHMS)

---

84 K. Stevenson, 'Thai war callit knychtis and bere the name and the honour of that hye ordre': *Scottish Knighthood in the Fifteenth Century The Fifteenth Century VI: Identity and Insurgency in the late Middle Ages* (Woodbridge, Boydell Press, 2006) p.36. Capwell, 'Observations on the armour...' p.6. There are of course a couple of outliers for example an effigy in Blackfriars graveyard in Inverness which may be the Earl of Mar who is wearing high status Lowland armour. Mar died in 1436 and what can be seen of the effigy appears to match that date.

85 In England, the Paston family famously rose from yeomen, although that in itself was a very broad term, to knights in a few generations. MacDonald, A, *The Kingdom of Scotland at War: 1332–1488*, p.175.

86 Capwell, T. E., 'Observations on the Armour...' p.5. Moffat, R. Dr, 'A hard harnest man': The armour of George Dunbar, 9th Earl of March', *Transactions of the East Lothian Antiquarian and Field Naturalists' Society* (North Berwick, Volume 30, 2015) pp.21–38, 496.

It is unfortunately quite difficult to date effigies precisely since although it is generally known whom the effigies depict and the date of their deaths.[87] What is not always known is at what point in the lifetime of the individual depicted by the effigy is being shown, e.g. whether he is carved as a warrior in his prime or as he was when he died – of course in some cases this may indeed be the same time.[88] However, one of the noticeable differences between the armour depicted in Scottish Lowland effigies and indeed the armour that appears in Scottish accounts in the 15th century is that the armour appears to be quite deliberately old fashioned in comparison with that of their contemporaries elsewhere.

The armour on the Lowland effigies would generally be dated as being from the first half of the 15th century if it were elsewhere.[89] It is particularly noticeable that for example the armour on the Lowland effigies lack tassets, which certainly seem to have been worn in most other places in Northern Europe by this period.[90] There is also no mention of them in the Treasurer's Accounts until after 1500 or much evidence elsewhere, e.g. in 1538 'Heir follow is Johne Deology … for twa elnis and half of crammosy sating … to be ane doublat of armes with tasslatis.'[91] It is unlikely that no Scots who could afford to import a harness in the latter part of the 15th century were not wearing tassets but that Scottish armourers do not seem to have been making armour with tassets until the sixteenth century.

There are mentions of sallets, which had become common all over Northern Europe after 1450, in the Treasurer's Accounts by 1490. 'That ilke gentilman haf and ten pundis worth of land or mare be … an armit with bassanat sellat quhyte [white] hat gorgeat or peissane hale leg harness werd spere and dager.'[92] However, as with England where they were imported from the Low Countries in large numbers, it is likely that merchants were bringing them into Scotland before this date from the Low Countries. Since unlike in England there are no examples of extant Scottish helmets and very few effigies from the latter part of the 15th century it is quite difficult to do as Dr Capwell has done for England and give an exact time line for the development of Scottish armour. Although, it does appear that the Scots continued to wear the bascinet with and without the attached aventail after

---

87   This is not always the case. The effigy in Dunkeld Cathedral of the 'Wolf of Badenoch, Alexander Stewart appears to date from roughly 1410–40. Stewart died in 1404/5 so this effigy while undoubtedly an elite man and probably a Stewart, may not be the Wolf of Badenoch.
88   T. Capwell, 'Observations on the Armour…' p.6. This is surprising, given that they date from the mid to late 15th century.
89   T. Capwell, 'Observations on the Armour', p.7.
90   See for example the effigy of Ross of Hawkwood dated to 1470, which has winged vambraces typical of the period but the rest of the harness looks early 15th century. He does not have any tassets, although of course the Highland Scots and the Irish weren't wearing them either.
91   1538 TA, VII p29
92   1491 RPS II 226/1

BOMBARDS, ENGINES, AND OTHER INSTRUMENTS OF WAR

the rest of Europe. 'Thre basnatis, price of the pece. Ilke gentilman … be sufficiently harnest & anarmit, with bassanat, sellat, quhyte hat, gorgeat.'[93]

Bascinets remained in use in England until at least the 1460s although becoming rarer as they were gradually replaced by sallets. The same happened in Scotland however it appears to have taken place more slowly judging from the frequency of the references to bascinets.[94]

Parliament however thought that enough men were wearing sallets as well as bascinets by 1456 to mention them in legislation. By 1507, the King was ordering a cap for his sallet. 'For ane elne rede bukram for ane how to the Kingis sellat' [for one ell red buckram for one cap the King his sellat].[95] It seems to have been quite common to cover helmets with a cap or bonnet, 'For ane bonet to the Kingis knapscaw.'[96] Knapskulls were often worn by common men as they were the simplest of helmets or for riding as here. 'For ij knapscallis to ryd wyth xijs.'[97] Armour was also often lined and covered with fabric – the type of fabric depended on the social status of the wearer much like the covering of a brigandine. 'Deliverit to Guilliame, armorar, to lyn the Kingis harnes, iij elnis dome grane' [grosgraine].[98] Some of the caps mentioned may have been worn as helmet linings or even as helmet substitutes, working class men may have worn padded coifs, although at this period unlike in the 16th century except in specific professions men did not wear linen coifs as part of their civilian headwear. The soldiers' coif was however a type of helmet made from cloth, sometimes leather or mail, or else the padding to be worn under the helmet.[99]

There are four English effigies dating from after 1450 that have great bascinets.[100] The effigy of Sir Nicholas Montgomery, St Andrew's Church, Derbyshire, which must date from at least 1462 since it has a livery collar for Edward IV, is very similar to many of the mid century or slightly later

Visored sallet, Flemish, circa 1475. (©Metropolitian Museum of Art)

---

93   "Basinet *n.*". *Dictionary of the Scots Language.* 2004. Scottish Language Dictionaries Ltd. Accessed 31 May 2021. RPS 1491/4/17. Date accessed: 2 May 2021. See also glossary
94   1508 TA IV p.121. 'To Will Raacutlellar, for...ane bar for ane basnet.'
95   1507 TA III, p.251.
96   1507 TA III, p.250.
97   1494 TA I 225
98   1532 TA VI. 30.
99   R. Moffat and M. Chambers, 'Armour: coif and capados/helmet linings', in: *Encyclopaedia of Medieval Dress and Textiles.*
100 T. Capwell, *Armour of an English Knight 1450–1500* (London, Thomas Del Mar Ltd, 2021), p.6.

effigies from Scotland.[101] Sir Nicholas is also wearing a bascinet, a knightly belt with plaques which continued to be worn in England into the 1460s so this is less old fashioned and these worn low over the fauld on almost all of the Scots effigies[102], 'A belt of crammasy [crimson] hernessit with gold.'[103] It is quite likely this had something to do with the strong chivalric culture that was in evidence at the Scots court where the wars of the 14th century were seen as the high point of Scots warrior culture.[104] James III took the sword of Robert the Bruce to Sauchieburn and probably his shirt also, 'King Robert Brucis serk.'[105] The effigy of Sir Nicholas also had a solid one-piece breastplate that was hinged on the left hand side and then strapped to the wearer's side on the right, again a feature of many of the Lowland effigies.

Several of the Scottish effigies also appear to have smooth breastplates as they were wearing a surcoat, or cote armour as it would have been called at the time.[106] Cote armour would often have had a heraldic design on it. It was tunic-like in form and made from an expensive fabric. 'For ij elne of dowbil rede taffaty, to be the Kingis cote armour'[107] The court painter, John Prat, was employed to paint the Arms on the King's cote armour and pavilions before his campaign in support of Perkin Warbeck, 'To Johne Pret, payntour, for paynting of pailʒoune thanis [pennants] and the kingis coete armour iij li.'[108] Pavilions of different sizes and sorts were taken on the raid on Ellen, including a hall, a kitchen and a closet. Men were also employed to take care of the tents.[109] They had also to make sure that the tents were not going to blow away in the north-east wind, 5s 4d; for taking a load of spikes (*laid of spakis*) from the castle to Holyrood to make tent pegs (*pailzoune pynnis*).[110] A few days later, two carts were carrying the tent poles (*pailzoun treis*) from Holyrood up the hill to the castle to put reinforcing bands on them and plates to stand the poles on (*bandis and platis*).[111]

In England, as elsewhere in Northern Europe the sallet was worn with a bevor. There are very few if any references to bevors in the Scottish records at this period although many to pisanes and gorgets. The word pisane was used to describe both a mail standard and an aventail. This suggests that bevors were not worn as much or that if worn they were imported

---

101 T. Capwell, Observations on The Armour...' p.7.
102 T. Capwell, Observations on The Armour...' p.9.
103 1488 TA I 83. Crammasy was normally velvet or satin.
104 K. Stevenson, 'Contesting Chivalry: James II and the control of chivalric culture in the 1450s', *Journal of Medieval History*, (London, Routledge, 2007) pp. 197–214.
105 TA Ip lxxiii
106 Ross of Hawkwood's effigy has cote armour on. R. Moffat, 'Coat Armour', *Encyclopaedia of Medieval Dress and Textiles*, Edited by: Gale Owen-Crocker, E. Coatsworth, M. Hayward. Consulted online on 26 May 2022 . Also, see glossary.
107 1496 TA I 296
108 1496 TA 1 297
109 Ibid I ccxxxiii
110 1496 TA I 289
111 Ibid I 290. A. Hodge, *Edinburgh Castle: The Medieval Documents* (Edinburgh, Historic Scotland, 2018).

as a piece with the sallet. Other pieces of mail like the standard were also worn to cover and protect any vulnerable areas. The mail pans, which were almost exactly what they sound like, mail breeches. Again, certainly elite men seem to have had lining for these which would make them not only more comfortable but also more long lasting – although the silk here while durable and long lasting may also be about showing off , just in the way that lining an arming doublet was 'iij quarteris of satyne to lyne his pans.'[112] The King also had sleeves of mail. 'To the King is sleiffis and pans of mail3e', which were presumably attached to an arming doublet. [113] These sleeves were also lined in satin, 'For i pair of arming schone of mail3ee.'[114] These were the mail ankle voiders worn under sabatons that can be seen on some English effigies, notably the effigy at Kedlestone dated 1460.[115]

Although the weapon of choice for the Scots had generally been a spear, many of the men had a variety of swords, particularly elite men. On the Lowland effigies, they appear to be mostly single-handed swords, these can be clearly seen on the effigies at Corstorphine Old Parish Church and this is reinforced by the Treasurers' Accounts. In them, in 1503, there is an order for a 'ridding suord and arming suord'.[116] It is probable that the riding sword was a falchion of sorts, a one handed single edged sword with a slight curve towards the end of the blade. The term arming sword or harness sword was used in the 15th and early 16th century to refer to a single-handed sword, 'For a harnas sword to the King.'[117] There were also two-handed long swords sometimes known as tucks from the French *étoc*. It was common for many of the sword blades to have been imported from the Low Countries and Germany and then mounted by armourers or sword slippers (although these terms were sometimes used inter-changeably) and dagger blades to have been made by cutlers. 'Bocht to the King fra the Franche cutlar, ij baslaris.'[118] However it is likely that some armourers finished or even made some blades themselves and they repaired them.[119] 'For dighting of viij suordis … agane Fastering is Evin [Shrove Tuesday] to the tournaying.'[120]

---

112   1495 TA I 295.
113   1496 Ib. 260.
114   1501 Ib. III. 22.
115   T. Capwell, *Armour of an English Knight*, p.106.
116   1503 TA III 124.
117   !496 TA I.
118   1495 TA I 227.
119   C. A. Whitelaw, S. Baxter, (eds) *Scottish Arms Makers: A Biographical Dictionary of Makers of Firearms, Edged Weapons and Armour Working in Scotland from the 14th Century to 1870* (London, Arms & Armour Press, 1977) p.17. Photos-Jones, 'Made in Scotland? Sword-Making in Scotland in the C15th & C16th in the Context of Recent Archaeological Evidence', in *Fields of Conflict: Progress & Prospect in Battlefield Archaeology*, P. W. M. Freeman and A. Pollard (eds) (Glasgow: Archaeopress, 2001), pp.61–72.
120   1505 TA. II. 476.

There are daggers on some of the effigies, these would have been produced by a cutler or blacksmith. 'For ane baislar with the kervit helf [carved handle], with gilt hilt and plomet [pommel]'.[121] 'That illk gentilman… be sufficandly harnest and anarmyt with…suerde, speir and dager.'[122] Robert Selkirk was the royal cutler from 1487 to 1512.[123] There were cutlers working throughout Lowland Scotland in Ayr, Dundee, Dunfermline, and Edinburgh as well as in Glasgow. A bollock dagger dated to 1500 was found at Coldingham Priory in the dig in the 1970s and is now at the National Museum of Scotland.[124]

Montgomery was also wearing a separate mail skirt the bottom of which could be seen under a breastplate fastened at the back. In this, he was very similar to the majority of the extant Lowland effigies and therefore it seems likely that so were the men who were present at Roxburgh and subsequent battles in Scotland.[125] Given Scotland's links with the Low Countries, Germany and France, elite men at least knew about and had access to the latest in helmet and armour design. Almost none of the later innovations that become common in armour elsewhere and may have been seen in Scotland (and indeed there's some evidence of this from account books) appear on these effigies.

There are a few other perhaps surprising aspects to some of the armour that was being worn in late 15th century Scotland. There were mentions for leg splints which are perhaps more characteristic of 14th century armour than of that of the 15th century. In an act of Parliament from 1430 those fighting were enjoined to, 'haif [a] pesane with brest plate, pans and legs splentis at the lest.'[126] Even in 1490, well after men in England had stopped wearing them, the Treasurers' Accounts record Muncur of Dundee being paid for 'leg splentis and a pare of arme splentis.' A few years later, he was also paid for 'ane pair of tourney gluffis and ane pair of inner gluffis [gloves].'[127] John Tait of Leith was paid for making 'a payre of harness to the King.'[128] In 1491, Parliament decreed that wappenschaws should be held four times a year. This law stated that a gentleman who had £10 worth of land should have a bascinet, sallet or a plain helmet – literally white or polished [bassanat, sellat quhyte hat.[129] Given that this was 1491 it is interesting that bascinets were still among the helmets specified.[130]

---

121 1503–4 TA II 223.
122 RPS 1425 II 10/2.
123 T. Caldwell. 'Royal Patronage of Arms and Armour', p.82.
124 Ibid p83, National Museum of Scotland 000–100–000–773-C
125 See Dr R. Moffat, 'A hard harnest Man' for a discussion of this.
126 RPS 1430 II /18/2.
127 1506 TA III, p.363.
128 1489 TA III
129 The pound Scots and sterling were probably worth the same in the 1360s, but the subsequent debasement of the pound Scots led to devaluation. The exchange rate was four pounds Scots to one pound English by the late 15th century.
130 RPS 1491/4/17. Accessed June 2021.

BOMBARDS, ENGINES, AND OTHER INSTRUMENTS OF WAR

One of the earliest mention of a brigandine in Scotland was in 1459 when payments were recorded as having being made to a Ligier/Legeyr, a Frenchman, who was a maker of brigandines, or 'lez briggandinis'.[131]. In 1462, he was paid for two ells of silk cloth called 'satyn figure' for a pair of brigandines for the King.[132] John Clement of Edinburgh was listed as being a brigandine maker in 1473.[133] Some fragments of the iron plates from a brigandine were found near Coldingham in the Borders in the early 1970s.[134] There is a late 15th century brigandine that has survived in Basel, which gives a good idea of what these brigandines were like. It was lined in red silk; remains of which were found under the rivet heads. The brigandine was made in a fashionable shape since elite men wore them not only for war but also for display.[135] Poorer men would probably have worn a jack [jak], made from layers of coarse undyed linen to provide them protection since they had little or no armour, 'ane jak with slevys to the hande'[136] Or more elite men frequently wore arming doublets with no padding to which their armour could then be attached:

> Vj [six] quarteris of quhitt reilȝe [literally white sackcloth]… to be the King a harnes doublet.[137]

Armour was attached with points:

> v dosane of grete hempin poyntis to the kingis harnes …v dosane of grete lethrin poyntis[138]

This sort of doublet was often made of rough linen or fustian, then lined sometimes with mail to protect the vulnerable armpits. Although very high status men might have them made with silk, satin or velvet in a display of conspicuous consumption, and then lined with linen or silk. In 1459 the Burgundian Antoine de la Sale suggested that tournament participants should wear a 'half-pourpoint of two toiles' ('*ung demi pourpoint de deux toilles*') under a brigandine, and over that cote armour.[139] In 1436: 'a delivery

---

131 ER, VI, 581.
132 ER, VII, 221 145.
133 C. A. Whitelaw, S. Baxter (eds), *Scottish Arms Makers*… p.62.
134 D. H. Caldwell, 'Fragments of a Brigandine from Coldingham Priory, Berwickshire', *The Proceedings of the Society of Antiquaries of Scotland*, volume 106, (Edinburgh, The Society of Antiquaries of Scotland, 1974–75) pp.219–21.
135 https://www.hmb.ch/en/museums/objects-in-the-collection/image-download/d/plate-mail-jacket/17712/ The brigandine is probably Italian and survived because it was wrongly attributed to Charles the Bold.
136 1456 RPS II 45/2.
137 1488 TA 1 265.
138 1495–6 TA I 262. The points are respectively made from hemp and leather.
139 L. Monnas, 'Pourpoint', *Encyclopaedia of Medieval Dress and Textiles*, Edited by: Gale

made by the wife of the accounter John Turing of two pipes and a cask' (*In duobus pipis et una rundella plenis harnesiis armorum*) full of harnesses of armour, and containing ten complete pairs of armour (*plenis harnesiis armorum, et continentibus decem paria armorum integra*), to Thomas Cranston, Constable of Edinburgh Castle to be put in the armoury (*locatis in armaria*) of the castle by the him, with the uncosts (additional expenses) at risk of the accounter, carried in the ship of Peter Dunkar, for twenty-five Flemish groats.[140] 'Gevin for a male harnes to the King.'[141] Just like the King in this instance many men particularly commoners would have fought in mail shirts rather than plate.

For a tournament in 1495, Perkin Warbeck had a parti-coloured hogton of white and purple damask, 'Purpour dammas, to be ane hogtoune to the Prince.' A hogton was normally sleeveless and often worn under mail. Parti-coloured clothes like these were mostly worn as livery. The colours suggest that King James was intent on making a statement about legitimacy of Warbeck's claim. It is unlikely that he actually believed that Warbeck was Prince Richard so this was done more as a piece of diplomatic gamesmanship rather than anything else. However, unlike in England purple was not reserved to the Royal family although in Treasurer's Accounts it is certainly more commonly worn by them than anyone else.[142] His six servitors had hogtons of tartar [silk] and gowns of damask, and his two trumpeters' gowns of Rowane tawny, hose of red kersey, and doublets of camlet, probably blue since murrey and blue were the Yorkist colours.[143]

The men from the Lowlands who were fighting in the latter part of the 15th century would have been dressed much the same as those in England or France. Scotland's court was heavily influenced by the Burgundian court, which meant that the elite by 1460 were wearing dark colours, if not black, following Burgundian fashion. Don Pedro de Ayala when visiting Scotland at the end of the 15th century said that, 'They spend all they have to keep up appearances. They are as well dressed as it possible to be in such a country.'[144] The colour of cloth was an important concern in Scots sumptuary legislation.[145] This concern with colour was in part to do with the cost and therefore prestige of the dye. The actual finishing costs were

---

Owen-Crocker, E. Coatsworth, M. Hayward. Consulted online on 26 May 2022
140 ER IV 680
141 1474 TA I 23
142 M. Hayward, 'Outlandish Superfluities': Luxury and Clothing in Scottish and English Sumptuary Law from the Fourteenth to the Seventeenth Century. G. Riello & U. Rublack (eds.), *The Right to Dress: Sumptuary Laws in a Global Perspective, c.1200–1800* (Cambridge: Cambridge University Press, 2019)pp. 96–120 at p.103.
143 1495 TA I 295. See also the glossary
144 P. Hume-Brown (ed.), *Early Travellers in Scotland* (Edinburgh, Nell& Co, 1891) p.44.
145 In the 1457/8, Commoners were limited to grey and white except on holy days, when they might wear light blue, green, or red.

the same regardless of the end colour.[146] Most of the more costly dyes were imported, although some – the brick reds, yellows and blue could be achieved more locally. The highest ranking of the men at court were given silk, typically taffeta, 'iij ellis of taftais to thare doublettis', and satin 'ij½ elne of sating … to be a doublat to the king.'[147] The Highland elite seemed to have been fond of satin which was made of silk at this time for doublets as well.

More middling rank men wore camlet (cammeloit) and woollen broadcloth. James II was depicted in a black short gown, wide brimmed hat, and long pointed fashionable shoes in the diary of Austrian nobleman Georg von Ehingen.[148] For Lent, Easter, and Whitsun of 1496 James IV was supplied with a riding gown, a syde [long] gown, a cloak, a short gown 'of the new fassoune', and a coat, all of Rijsel black.[149] The long gown needed four or five ells of cloth to make. The nobility and gentry of Scotland dressed similarly showing their elite status with dark, rich colours, 'For ij elne of murray claytht in grayne to be him a lang gown.'[150] The same colours dominate the wardrobe of Henry VIII, with black items of clothing appearing frequently in the accounts.[151] They were often lined in fur 'V mantill of banis [probably beaver] to lyne a syde gowne to the King.'[152] Or a 'bred and a half or bwge' [a breadth and a half of buge, that is lambskin fur which was very highly prized.][153] The sumptuary laws limited commoners to grey and white, which in practice probably meant retaining the natural colour of the wool – except on holy days when they could wear light blue, green or red.[154] All relatively cheap and easily obtainable dyes although this depended of course on the quality of the wool, the mordant used and the dye. In England, the contemporary poet John Gower looked back nostalgically to the days when labourers wore plain grey.[155] In the sumptuary law of 1429 yeomen and the

---

146 J. Munro, 'The anti-red shift – to the 'Dark Side': Colour changes in Flemish luxury woollens, 1300 – 1550', *Medieval Clothing and Textiles*, volume 3, No. 1 2007, pp.55–98.
147 1494 TA I 233.1473 TA. I 15.
148 *The Diary of Jörg von Ehingen*, M. Letts (ed.), (London, Oxford University Press, 1929), pp.62–3.
149 R. Marshall, "To be the Kingis Grace ane Dowblett': The Costume of James V, King of Scots', *Costume 28* (1994), p.14. A gown of the new fasshone would be a short gown with wider sleeves rather than a longer one. Rijsel is the Flemish name for Lille, so wool that comes from Lille.
150 Murrray is a purple/red. The cloth will have been dyed blue then over dyed with kermes (the in grayne), an expensive imported dye. This was a very high status garment.
151 M. Hayward, 'Crimson, Scarlet, Murrey and Carnation: Red at the Court of Henry VIII', *Textile History 38:2*, November 2007, p.141.
152 1473 TA I 15. Mantils were 60 skins. NB, 'syde' means long.
153 1488 TA I 137
154 F. Shaw, 'Sumptuary Legislation in Scotland', *Judicial Review 24. 1979* p.82, (Edinburgh, Edinburgh University Press).
155 J. Lee, *The Medieval Clothier*, (Woodbridge, S Boydell & Brewer, 2018) p.12. The grey cloth in Scotland was of course what would later in the 16th century what would come to be known as 'hodden grey'. A plain weave wool such as 'russet or

common people were forbidden from wearing coloured clothes reaching below the knee [*hat na ȝeman wer hewyt clathes siddar na the kne*],[156] as well clothes that were '*ragyt*' which in this context meant slashed – this applied to the country or 'landward' people.

The sumptuary laws of 1457 restricted merchants from the wearing of silk and costly scarlet. 'That na man…that levys be merchandice bocht and thare wifis weire claiths of silk nor costly scarlatis in gownys.'[157] The concern of sumptuary legislation was twofold; in part it was an attempt by the government to encourage spending on Scottish goods rather than imported silks, fine linens and dyes. Equally important though was controlling the clothing of the aspirant middle classes and nouveau rich bourgeoisie who the changing social and economic conditions of the 15th century had allowed to develop more wealth and as such in their dress it could be impossible to distinguish from their social betters.

It is reasonable to assume that this amount of effort to control the dress of the commons meant that the Government felt that they were prone to extravagance. In 1471, sumptuary legislation had restricted the wearing of silk fabrics to knights, minstrels, heralds, high-ranking burgesses, and those with £100 of annual rent.[158] Although this is a book primarily about the dress of men for obvious reasons it is worth noting that Scottish sumptuary laws were inclusive in their restrictions in that unlike in England where the legislation was very much focused around men, the Scots Parliament also wanted to make sure that women didn't wear clothing inappropriate to their station.

The lists of fabrics banned for most people, or restricted to the elite, by the 1581 sumptuary law, show the wide varieties available – cloth of gold and silver, 'ane cote to the King, half chekkrit with claith of gold,'[159] velvet, satin 'graith [to make] to a doublat of red crammacy [crimson] satin'[160]; damask, reid [red] dammysk for a gowne to the Duke,[161] and taffeta (this was made of silk at this time) and at the raid of Norham in support of Perkin Warbeck, the King's henchmen were wearing red taffeta coats over their doublets. The King wore a coat of Kendal green.[162] 'For vij [seven] elne of grene kentdalee, to be ane cote to the King' - Kendal green was a rough

'hodden'. These woollen fabrics were very popular with the working classes and were frequently used for hose, wyliecoats, gowns, jackets and coats. They were associated strongly with the 'country' or rural working classes. They were woven from the undyed sheep's wool, which could be anything from white (quhite), grey or brown/black because of the natural colour of sheep's wool.

156   1429 RPS II 18/2.
157   RPS 1457/II/49/2.
158   *RPS*, 1471/5/7. Date accessed: 16 May 2022.
159   F. Shaw, 'Sumptuary Legislation in Scotland', p.84. 1508 TA IV. 24.
160   1473 TA I 15.
161   1488 TA I 153.
162   1497 TA I 340.

frieze cloth. It is possible given the size of the coat that this may have been intended for the King to wear over his armour.

The King had a hood and mittens of French black wool made for him. 'Two pairs of '*quhit hos*', his mittens were also lined in white and he had a jacket of cloth of gold from eight ells of silk. His hood had a tippet or *tepatis* from silk. He also had a cap and 'singil [cloth] bonat'[163] for his sallet. This implies a cap for protection, whether knitted and fulled or padded linen and then a wool bonnet over the helmet. This gives a rare glimpse of cold weather clothes, clearly the majority of the men would not have been wearing a jacket of cloth of gold however many of the men would have worn hoods and mittens and 'bonats'. An Aberdeen judgement of assize in 1446, listed Sandy Voket, a burgess in the town as having a 'best goune and best hude', which also suggested that he had more than one jacket or gown that he might have worn.[164]

'Al nakit bot sark breke,' [All naked but shirt and breeches].[165] The white linen sarks or shirt necklines that the King and his henchmen wore would have been large enough to slip over the head, sometimes especially towards the end of the century they had a straight collar. A fastening of any kind at the neck and sleeve was uncommon.[166] The colour and quality of the linen was dependent on social status, and thus, the elite, like the King had shirts made from fine white linen from the Netherlands, 'xvj elne of Hollande clathe for sarkis.'[167] He also had kerchiefs made of the same fine linen made for wearing round his neck. 'ij elne of Holland clayth to brest curcheis.'[168]

James IV in 1495 had shirts made in the new fashion. These shirts would have been cut with a straight collar. The King's shirts were sewn with silk thread. In contrast to this poor men had unbleached linen made locally.[169]

---

163   1502 TA II 198. The mittens would have been made of cloth and two fingered. These very commonly worn by working class men for working in cold weather. There are examples of knitted mittens for children in the sixteenth century.

164   E. Gemmill, 'Debt, Distraint, Display and Dead Men's Treasure: Material Culture in Late Medieval Aberdeen', *Journal of Medieval History* (Amsterdam, Elsevier, 2020) pp.350–372 at p.21.

165   Breke *n.*". *Dictionary of the Scots Language*. 2004. Scottish Language Dictionaries Ltd. Accessed 12 May 2021. This particular reference to underwear is from 1400 but there's no reason to suppose that the word or practice had changed except in that the underwear became shorter and tighter as doublets also became shorter and tighter and hose went from being single legged to joined in the middle of the century for all but the poorest and even they were wearing joined hose by the latter part of the century in the Lowlands.

166   S. Thursfield, 'Underwear – a historical overview', *Encyclopaedia of Medieval Dress and Textiles of the British Isles 450–1450*, G. Owen-Crocker, E. Coatsworth, M. Hayward (Eds). Consulted online on 07 January 2022 (Leiden, Brill, 2012).

167   1490 TA I 190.

168   Ib 190.

169   For example, 'To gif to Blynd Jame – a hardin sark', from "Hardin *n., adj.*", *Dictionary of the Scots Language*. 2004. Scottish Language Dictionaries Ltd. Accessed 14 Aug 2022. Later this was also controlled in the sumptuary laws. Scotland specialised in the production of coarse lower end linen, which meant

Over their mid-thigh length shirts all men wore tight woollen hose that came to the hip. As ever, the elite had more elaborate hose, sometimes with slashes on the knee in darker colours. 'For … Fransche blak to ii pairs party hoyse to the king.'[170] His henchmen, which in this context just meant the men around the king rather than the more sinister modern meaning had 'reid carsay to be ix pairs of hoyse.'[171] Kersey, an English cloth that was ideal for hose since it stretched well if cut on the diagonal or bias. Also made of the same good English kersey were 'cayrsay to be x payres chort hoyse.'[172] These were sometimes called sokkis or fute [foot] sokes and worn over the full-length hose to protect them. They were often worn with riding boots and were sometimes made of linen. 'For quhit [white] clath to be sokkis to the King.'[173] In 1496, the King, for his expedition to the Isles, had a pair of 'hose to the knee,' made, which were breeches cut tight to the leg and worn with cloth short hose on the lower legs.[174]

By the end of the 15th century, men often wore a petticoat [a little coat] or wyliecoat made from wool to which they pointed their hose and wore under their doublets, prior to that their hose had been laced to the doublets, 'j elne of skarlete for a petticote to the king.'[175] Wyliecoats frequently matched the hose. These were certainly being worn by the late 1470s.[176] In 1488, 'reid cayrsay [red kersey] to be a wylecoyt and hoyse' bought for the middling servants.[177] Every man wore a doublet that would often match the colour of the hose and as with the hose, the elite wore darker richer colours and fabrics, 'Kingis dowblat of blac vellous.' At the raid of Norham, in 1496, the henchmen of James IV wore coats of red taffeta and doublets of black fustian.[178] The middling sorts and servants had paler colours and less expensive fabric. 'For xiii elne of fusteane to be doubletis to ix hensmen.'[179] Hose were laced to doublets or wyliecoat with points, 'iiij dussane of poyntis to thir saim hoyse.'[180] The sumptuary law of 1430 forbade the wearing of 'embroidery nor pearl nor bullion', evidentially to stop people from making relatively plain clothes look higher status with the judicious application of pearls or passementerie.[181]

---

high quality linen was generally going to be imported.
170 1489 TA I 149.
171 1488 TA 1 173.
172 1488 Ib 156.
173 1498 TA 1 298.
174 1495 TA I 225.
175 1474 Ib 26. Scarlet being both a cloth and a colour.
176 "Wylecot *n*.". *Dictionary of the Scots Language*. 2004. Scottish Language Dictionaries Ltd. Accessed 21 Aug 2021.
177 1488 TA I 157.
178 1497 TA I clxxvii.
179 1488 TA I 164.
180 1490 TA I 149.
181 M. Hayward, 'Outlandish Superfluities', p.112, *RPS*, 1430/12. Date accessed: 2 October 2021

BOMBARDS, ENGINES, AND OTHER INSTRUMENTS OF WAR

Liveries were distributed for the most part to the Scottish Royal Household and in many other great households in December, the period of preparation for Christmas and New Year, as this was the traditional time to give gifts.[182] 'The xvj [16th] day of December beginnyn to giff lyverayis, [liveries] in the first for v elne Franch blak to Schir Peter Crechtoun.'[183] Until the reign of James V (1513–42) there were no fixed livery colours for the Scottish King's household however here as elsewhere they were wearing distinctive colours – 'chamlet, rede and quhite, [white] to be ilkain of thame a liffray pe.'[184] A livery pe was a rough coat, probably worn for riding or over other clothes. Although a gentleman might wear something more like a journay. 'To the King agane his passage in the Ilis … ij ellis of crammesy vellous [crimson velvet], to be a jurenay abone his harness.'[185] A kind of cloak specifically cut for wearing over armour and was mostly decorative. He also had a sea coat made for this journey and a 'greit hud of Rowan tawny' lined with lambskin. Lining gowns and hoods with fur was common, however sumptuary laws forbade the wearing of rich furs by those who were not of the nobility or part of the King's household although unlike in England sable was not confined to royalty.[186] An act of the 1430 Parliament banned the wearing of 'furs of pine-martens, beech-martens, purray nor great or richer furs' and in 1457, 'the clerks, that none wear gowns of scarlet or marten fur, except if he is a person constituted in dignity in cathedral or collegiate churche.'[187] Hoods were at this time worn by travellers and sometimes men working outside thus some of the common soldiers in the royal army are likely to have worn a less luxurious hood.[188] James IV wore a velvet cloak for the raid of Ellem in 1496. It was made from 18 ells of velvet, lined with the same amount of satin.[189] Silks at this time were only 20 to 22 inches wide so while this is a very large amount of fabric for what was presumably a circular cloak it's not quite as huge as it first appears.

The fashionable men in the 1460s were wearing poulaines with pointed toes. James II is depicted as wearing them in the image that appears in the diary of Austrian nobleman Georg von Ehingen. The sabatons worn with armour mirrored the appearance of these shoes until both the shoes and sabatons changed profile and became wider and flatter in profile. Poulaines dropped out of fashion and in the latter part of the century, the men were wearing square-toed shoes, short boots and high boots [brodikynnis], 'To

---

182 TA, 1, pp.473 clxxvi-clxxvii.
183 1505 TA III 104 Schir was.
184 1494 TA I 233.
185 1494 TA I 226.
186 M. Hayward, 'Outlandish Superfluities', p.103.
187 M. Hayward, 'Outlandish Superfluities', p.107. 'Pured' white miniver, white fur taken from the winter coat of a grey squirrel (*OED*), RPS, 1430/12. RPS, 1458/3/14. Date accessed: 2 October 2021.
188 Rowan was the name for Rouen. Tawney was a reddish brown colour.
189 1496 TA I 261.

Jame Lyntoune, for schvne, brodikynnis and butis.'[190] These longer boots were generally worn for riding.

It is worth noting that many of the men within the King's household were gentlemen or nobility in their own right so on the battlefield would wear coat armour displaying their colours or arms. The 14th century Caerlaverock Roll, contains a description of a dispute between two knights who had the same Arms so clear identification was important not just to protect you from the enemy.[191] There would often be heralds who would also wear heraldry. They were exempt from the sumptuary laws that restricted the wearing of silk to a knight with an income of £100. Therefore, their coat armour was made of 'double taffeta' or 'tartar'. Other men in a household would wear the clothes that they had appropriate to their station – livery in this context simply means clothing or cloth that retainers were given, it was sometimes but not always distinctive. This was also the case in other great men's households.

The clothing that men wore on and around the battlefield was not uniform nor was it yet a uniform for all that there were sometimes badges or bends or even sometimes but not always and not for everyone coats or other items of clothing in the same colours. There was also a mixture of fabric types used in livery, including velvet, fustian, kersey, taffeta, and camlet depending on social class of the recipient. Master gunners often received black livery showing their status within the court.[192] Blue clothes or cloth were often given to servants and soldiers since it was a cheap and easily obtainable colour, so much so that by the 16th century gentlemen generally wouldn't wear blue as it had become associated with servants, apprentices, soldiers or the poor. 'To xiij ȝemen [yeoman] of the Kingis and the Queynis, to thare lyvera govnis at the parliament, xviii elne of blew.'[193] An example of this, are the Bedesmen of Aberdeen and Edinburgh who were poor men who prayed for the souls of their benefactors, as part of their uniform or livery they wore a distinctive blue cloak.[194]

---

190 1494 TA I 223.
191 R. Jones, *Bloody Banners...*, p.24.
192 1496 TA I 296.
193 1474 Ib 64.
194 R. McAleese, 'Aberdeen's Bedesmen: Poverty and Piety', (*History Scotland*, Jan/Feb 2012), pp. 46–49.

3

We carried war-raiment and Arms

> The ancient way of fighting was by set battles; and for arms some had broad two-handed swords and head-pieces, and others Bows and Arrows.[1]

Throughout late medieval Europe, the aristocracy and the monarchy shared a common value system in which individual valour and success in battle was rewarded and prized.[2] The Highlands and Isles of Scotland were part of this shared culture despite Walter Bower's assertion that all Highlanders were basically barbarians.[3] In 1456, James II presented a silver royal livery collar to the Lord of the Isles' half-brother, Gill Easbuig [Celestine] of the Isles.[4]

---

1 M. Martin, *A Description of the Western Islands of Scotland* (Edinburgh, The Mercat Press, 1982), p.210.

2 There does not seem to have been a specifically Scottish chivalric elite order in the 15th century but in all other respects Scots martial culture celebrated the knightly warrior. K. Stevenson, 'The Unicorn, St Andrew and the Thistle: Was There an Order of Chivalry in Late Medieval Scotland?' *The Scottish Historical Review*, vol. 83, no. 215, (Edinburgh University Press,2004), p.6. M. A. Penman, 'Christian Days and Knights: the Religious Devotions and Court of David II of Scotland, 1329–71', *Historical Research*, volume 75, no 189, 2002, pp.249–272, at pp.261–265

3 Martin MacGregor, 'Gaelic Barbarity and Scottish Identity in the later Middle Ages', Broun, Dauvit and MacGregor, Martin (eds.) *Mìorunmòr nan Gall, 'The great ill-will of the Lowlander'? Lowland perceptions of the Highlands, medieval and modern.* (Centre for Scottish and Celtic Studies, University of Glasgow, Glasgow 2009), pp.7–48. In fact, the view from elsewhere had all Scots as hairy and uncouth – despite all evidence to the contrary. A calumny that has proven difficult for the Scots to shake off in the last 600 years.

4 This livery collar is likely to have had a unicorn on it. K. Stevenson, 'Contesting Chivalry: James II and the control of chivalric culture in the 1450s', *Journal of Medieval History*, (London, Routledge, 2007) pp. 197–214, at p.200.

THE MEN OF WARRE

West Highland warrior, from Iona Abbey. An effigy of a man wearing armour. On his head, which rests on a pillow, he wears a mail coif and a bascinet. He also wears an aketon. He has a sword on his left side. (© RCHAMS)

The fortunate survival of a considerable body of sculpture, which includes many complete effigies in the West Highlands, provides evidence of the shared martial culture that underpinned elite society there. The effigies and grave slabs depict warriors in light armour with a bascinet, a padded aketon/actoun in Scots [cotin in Gaelic] and frequently holding a sword, spear or great axe.[5] Other symbols of military power often shown on the graves include bows and arrows, galleys, and castles.[6]

The majority of the warfare in the Highlands and Isles of Scotland took place on foot, partly because of the importance of the sea to their culture, but also for the purely practical reason that there was little suitable grazing in most of the Highlands that could keep a horse alive throughout the year; this is in direct contrast to Ireland where the horse was very important to warfare. Although there was legislation from 1424 that stated that all gentlemen with an income of more than £20 Scots should have a suitable horse 'as a gentleman ought to'.[7] However vital to the martial culture of the West Highlands was the presence of the Galloglass, the elite warrior class. In the later medieval period, the Isles were the source of the Galloglass literally foreign warrior [gall-òglach] who campaigned in Ireland as mercenary warriors and bodyguards; originally they were only associated with the North of Ireland however by the latter part of the 15th century they were also in Munster and Leinster.[8] One English observer commented that they did 'not leave the field lightly but rather bide the brunt to the death.'[9] Martin says that the Galloglass were the chief's bodyguard in the Isles, 'every Chieftain had a bold Armour-Bearer, whose Business was always to attend the Person of his Master Night and Day … and this Man was called Galloglach.'[10]

There were also the caterans, landless men who probably served for plunder rather than pay when fighting in Ireland. They would have also made up the majority of any Highland fighting force in Scotland and

---

5 T. E. Capwell, 'Observations on the Armour…' p.5.
6 R. M. Crawford, *Warfare in the West Highlands and Isles of Scotland, c. 1544–1615*, (Glasgow, unpublished PhD thesis, 2016), p.33.
7 Quoted in M. Hayward, 'Outlandish Superfluities', p.117.
8 Simms, K. *'From Kings to Warlords'* (Woodbridge, Boydell Press, 2000) p124. Galloglass means foreign warrior
9 T. Willis, 'The Scottish Two Handed Sword', p.14.
10 M. A. Martin, *A Description of the Western Islands*, p.104.

would have been far less well armed and equipped than the elite men, 'Gif ony cumpany, catherane, or punʒeoun of lymmaris, risi in the cuntre to makbrek, reif' [Give any company caterans or a small group of rogues who rise in the country to make break, plunder].[11] Highlanders with experience of fighting in Ireland would have more familiarity with warfare than the majority of any Royal army.[12] Highlanders were present at the siege of Roxburgh in 1460, in James IV's campaign in the north of England in 1490s, Flodden in 1513 and Pinkie Cleugh in 1547.[13]

The book of the Dean of Lismore, which was compiled in the first half of the 16th century in eastern Perthshire, describes aristocratic Highland men:

> *Do bhiodh eideadh agus ainn ag dul linn do sheilg mar soin;*
> *ni bhiodh feinnidh dhiobh im dhoigh gan leinidh shroill is da choin.*
> *Gan chotun sithe seimli, gan luirigh sparrtha ghcir ghloin,*
> *gan chcinnbheirt chlochordha chorr, 's a dha shlcigh i ndom gach fir.*
> [We carried war-raiment and arms whenever we so went hunting.
> I believe there was no warrior amongst them without a satin tunic and two hounds;
> Without a soft smooth wadded tunic and a clinched corselet sharp and bright,
> a rounded jewelled and gilded helmet, and his two spears in each man's hand].[14]

Warfare in the Highlands and Isles at this time took place in relatively small, set piece battles. Descriptions of battles in both the Highlands and Ireland suggest that there were relatively low numbers of armoured men. As elsewhere hunting was seen as a way to practise war . Men who hunted and fought were the elite of Gaelic society:

> The other part of these people delight in the chase and a life of indolence ; their chiefs eagerly follow bad men if only they may not have the need to labour; taking no pains to earn their own livelihood,

---

11 "Cateran *n.*". *Dictionary of the Scots Language*. 2004. Scottish Language Dictionaries Ltd. Accessed 13 Sep 2021
12 G. Phillips, 'Scotland in the Age of Military Revolution, 1488–1560', J. A. Crang, E. M. Spiers & M. J. Strickland, (Eds), *A Military History of Scotland*, (Edinburgh, Edinburgh University Press, 2014) pp.182–207 at p.184
13 M. MacGregor, 'Warfare in Gaelic Scotland in the Later Middle Ages',), *A Military History of Scotland*, (Edinburgh, Edinburgh University Press, 2014) p.212
14 Quoted in A. E. M. Wiseman, 'Chasing the Deer, Hunting Iconography and Tradition in the Scottish Highlands', (Edinburgh, 2007, unpublished PhD) p.31. 'Leinidh shroill' can be literally translated as 'satin shirt' but it can also be translated as a tunic, which is more likely in this context. So this may actually be a doublet or a tunic.

they live upon others, and follow their own worthless and savage chief in all evil courses sooner than they will pursue an honest industry. They are full of mutual dissensions, and war rather than peace is their normal condition.'[15]

Lowland 16th century historians loved Gaelic Scots' devotion to hunting as it was warfare by any other means and they saw therefore the Highlanders as retaining virtues that the Lowlanders were losing.[16]

Much of the sculpture implies that many if not most of the fighting men did not wear a mail shirt and the long padded cotin or actoun was their only protection. They appear to be made from linen and quilted vertically in long narrow rolls. The jacks with long sleeves mentioned in the Acts of Parliament in 1456 are at least very similar to aketons as are the jacks referred to in the later act of 1481.[17]

Aketons are also referred to in the Acts of Parliament 'That … evir ilk lawyt [this means laity but in this context is actually common] man … salhaf … a gud suffyciand acton, a basnet, and gluffis of playt.'[18] Aketons were similar to a jack but were normally, as in the example at Ardchattan, tailored in at the waist and worn to the knee rather than the waist.. They seem to have fastened up the front. There's one effigy at Oronsay where the buttons can be seen down the front.[19] Some had a slit at the front, which could be for sitting on a horse. Gauntlets [*gluffis of plat*] are represented on some effigies as are spurs but until the later effigies where they are shown in plate armour there is no leg protection. It is likely that some of the Highland men were also wearing aketons that were covered in leather, Hector Boece in his History of Scotland, translated in 1533 describes 'sing bow and scheif, licht harnes, habergeouns, sum of ime, sum of leddir, commonly callitn actouns.'[20]

The 16th century Scots historian, John Major describes:

The wild Scots…war rather than peace is their natural condition… From Mid leg to the foot they go uncovered: their dress is for an over garment a loose plaid and for a shirt saffron dyed. They are armed with bow and arrows, a broadswords and a small halbert. They

---

15   J. Major, *A History…* p.49.
16   M. MacGregor, *Warfare in Gaelic Scotland*, p.211
17   D. H. Caldwell, 'Having the Right Kit: West Highlanders', S. Duffy (ed.), *The World of the Galloglass: Kings, Warlords and Warriors in Ireland and Scotland 1200–1600* (Dublin, Four Courts Press, 2007, 2016) pp.144–168 at p.155.
18   "Gluve n.". *Dictionary of the Scots Language*. 2004. Scottish Language Dictionaries Ltd. Accessed 17 Sep 2021.
19   J. W. M. Steer & K. A. Bannerman, *Late Medieval Monumental Sculpture*, p.112.
20   J. W. M. Steer & K. A. Bannerman, *Late Medieval Monumental Sculpture*, p.155. G. Watson, *The Mar Lodge Translation of the History of Scotland by Hector Boece.*(Edinburgh, Scottish Text Society. Third Series, volume 17, 1946), p.50.

WE CARRIED WAR-RAIMENT AND ARMS

always carry in their belt a stout dagger single edged, but of the sharpest. In time of war they cover the whole body with a coat of mail made of iron rings and in it they fight. The common folk amongst the wild Scots go out to battle in a linen garment sewed together in patchwork

(this is probably a jack that has been strengthened by linen threads rather than patchwork which is not a contemporaneous concept) well daubed with wax or pitch and with an overcoat of deerskin.[21] Two of the effigies at Iona might also be dressed in deerskin garments[22], and additionally, the galloglass in Ireland are described as wearing padded leather jacks.[23]

The type of sword carried by the elite men fighting in the Highlands in the early and mid 15th century is clearly depicted on the de Greenlaw monument from the battle of Harlaw in 1411. It was larger than earlier swords, almost a hand and half size. Other examples can be seen on contemporary gravestones all over the west coast and elsewhere in Scotland – for example, on the tomb of Mackenzie of Kintail, Beauly Priory.[24] There is an extant half-lang sword that matches these depictions in the collection of Glasgow Museums at Kelvin Grove and another in the collection of the Art Museum at Philadelphia.[25]

The Scottish sword slippers and lorimers attached the blades which were mostly imported from Germany to the distinctive hilts with spoon shaped quillons on the cross guard which drop gently towards the blade. The blades of the swords were wider and heavier than previous swords, and double-edged being made for cutting as well as thrusting.[26] Scottish smiths and armourers were for the most part not able to produce enough blades of this size, quality or quantity to satisfy demand although there is some evidence that some swords were made in Scotland. 'Five pair of halflang hiltis' are listed in the goods left by an Edinburgh lormier.[27]

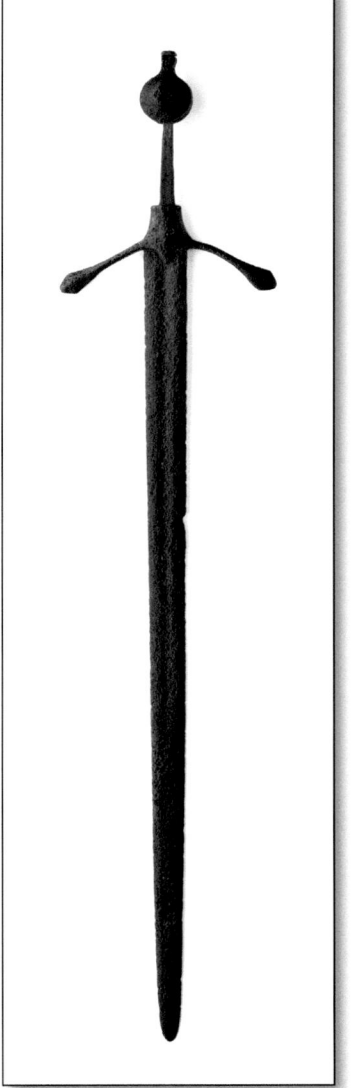

This is an extremely rare surviving example of a type of sword carried by Scottish knights. A similar sword is represented on a funeral monument believed to be that of Robert de Greenlaw (died 1411) at Kinkell, Aberdeenshire, Scotland. (© Philadelphia Art Museum)

---

21 J. Major, (A. Constable, ed.) *A History of Greater Britain as well England as Scotland* (Edinburgh, Scottish History Society, 1892), p.49.
22 J. Major, (A. Constable, ed.) *A History of Greater Britain as well England as Scotland* (Edinburgh, Scottish History Society, 1892), p.159.
23 K. Simms, *From Kings to Warlords*, (Woodbridge, Boydell Press, 2000) p.125.
24 R. Moffat, 'A Sign of Victory?: 'Scottish Swords' and Other Weapons in the Possession of the 'Auld Innemie', (London, Arms & Armour, 2000) pp.122–139 at p.125.
25 http://collections.glasgowmuseums.com/mwebcgi/mweb?request=record;id=150237;type=101. Thanks to Paul MacDonald for pointing this out. Scottish longsword, Philadelphia Museum of Art, Von Kienbusch bequest, 1977.
26 T. Willis, *The Scottish Two Handed Sword*, p.35.
27 *Edinburgh Testaments, 1514–32, 1567–1700*, MS NAS CC8/8/1–80, 80 volumes. A Hutchison died in 1577.

At the end of the 15th century the half-lang began to be less popular although it did not disappear. It is at this point that transitional claymores appear in carvings and elsewhere. Perhaps the best examples are on an inscribed slab dated 1495 at Cladh Beg, Kirkapoll on Tiree and the sword held by the effigy of Alexander MacLeod at Rodel.[28]

Javelins and darts are mentioned in some documents of the mid 16th century, javelins were not necessarily for throwing as in the modern sense of the word. In his letter to Henry VIII, John Elder claimed that the 'Highland Scots…delite and pleasure…in rynninge, leapinge, swymmynge, shootynge, and thrawinge of dartis.'[29] In the 16th century, Bishop Leslie's *Historie of Scotland* stated that in 1540, two great ships were sent from France by James V as a gift, loaded with 'speir and Javeling, darte and arrow, Gun and geinzie [crossbow bolts] with all kynd of armour'.[30] Barbour in the early 15th century mentions darts 'With alkyne instrument of were, As gyne, slonge, darte and spere.'[31] Sir John Dowdall, at the siege of Enniskillen in 1596, described the Scots as fighting in Ireland 'with stones, casting spears and galloglass axes, as they have been accustomed.'[32]

The armour typically worn in the West Highlands can be seen by looking at effigies such as that of Somerled MacDougall and his son at Ardchattan Priory, Argyllshire. The earlier effigy dating from the late 15th century is bearded. His bascinet has a very pointed helm similar to images seen on Irish tombs of a similar date and Gilbride McKinnon at Iona.[33] It has border of raised rings above the face opening. A large aventail falls over the shoulders to a point down the chest.[34] The aketon, which is tailored in at the waist, reaches well down the legs.[35]

Another aketon can be seen on the mid 15th century Macmillan cross at Knapdale commemorating Alexander Macmillan, keeper of Castle Sween. The huntsman on the cross is wearing a knee length gown, a large hood with a long liripipe, possibly gloves and is holding a large battle axe.[36] There

---

28 T. Willis, *The Scottish Two Handed Sword*, p.45.
29 *The Bannatyne Miscellany* (Edinburgh, 1827), p.13.
30 J. Leslie, Bishop of Ross, *The Historie of Scotland written first in Latin and translated in Scottish by Father Dalrymple* E. G. Cody (ed.), 2 volumes., Edinburgh, 1885–95.
31 "Dart n.". *Dictionary of the Scots Language*. 2004. Scottish Language Dictionaries Ltd. Accessed 11 Sep 2021 <http://www.dsl.ac.uk/entry/dost/dart_
32 R. Moffat, 'A Sign of Victory?', p.132.
33 There are many examples of this. For example, the effigy of a warrior at Kilmartin Parish Church, Argyll who wears a pointed bascinet with a large aventail, an aketon which probably fastens at the front, a broad sword rather than a claymore and has a spear in his other hand. Kilmory Parish church has another effigy.
34 J. W. M. Steer & K. A. Bannerman, *Late Medieval Monumental Sculpture In The West Highlands* (Edinburgh, The Royal Commission on the Ancient & Historical Monuments of Scotland, 1977) pp.27–9.
35 Making it very similar to the aketon worn in the drawing by Durer dated 1521.
36 A. E. M. Wiseman, *Chasing the Deer, Hunting Iconography and Tradition in the Scottish Highlands* (Edinburgh, University of Edinburgh 2007, unpublished PhD

is a man without armour depicted on the cross at Kilmory Parish Church, Isle of Arran who is wearing a similar gown to the huntsman. His gown is belted at the waist, has puffed sleeves with narrow cuffs, and possibly braid with a herringbone pattern on the hem. He seems to be wearing a dagged hood that covers his neck and shoulders and on his head is a hat with a pronounced roll round the brim.

Alexander Macleod's Hunting scene (© RCHAMS)

The effigies of MacLeod Chiefs at Rodel Church, Harris, show the development of West Highland armour. Alexander MacLeod's effigy shows him in traditional West Highland armour; with a long actoun, a bascinet with a prominent helm, a large aventail and his sword looks very much like a West Highland claymore in size and shape.[37] Men in the West Highlands continued to favour mail into the 16th century as it suited the way that they fought. One of the key reasons for this is that guns didn't make their way into Highland battles until later in the 16th century.[38] William MacLeod and John Macleod both wear plate armour as became common for elite men in the Highlands in the latter part of the 16th century. John carries

---

    thesis) p.33.
37   See T. Willis, *The Scottish Two Handed Sword* for a further discussion of this.
38   M. MacGregor, *Warfare in Gaelic Scotland*, p.224.

a fully-fledged claymore. Over a period of approximately 30 years these detailed effigies show how the West Highland claymore evolved into its final two-handed form by the middle of the 16th century.

There were two types of shields used by Scots at this period – bucklers and targes. An act of Parliament in 1456 stated that:

> each man whose goods extend to 20 merks be furnished with..a sword and a buckler, a bow and a sheaf, and if he can not shoot that he shall have an axe and a targe either of leather or of board with two hands on the back.[39]

At the Parish Church at Kellis there are two slabs showing bucklers from the late 15th century one with a sword belt and both with swords with lobated [leaf-shaped pommels], slightly sloped quillons and a scabbard-chap.[40] Bucklers, which were small round shields, were of course not unique to Highlanders, men in the Lowlands also had bucklers. 'Ane buklar and ane swerd belt to the King'[41]. The former are small and circular and have a handle for the left hand. They were used along with swords, and were called for in legislation of 1425/6, 1429/30, 1456 and 1491. Targes are also mentioned in the legislation and appear in the Treasurers' Accounts, for example in 1513, three score targes [a score is 20, so 60] were bought for the Royal Navy, 'Johne Watson, smyth…thre skor of targes.'[42]

The Books of Clanranald are two manuscripts that date to around the early 18th century. They are written in Classical Gaelic, and are collections of earlier documents. The books contain many descriptions of warriors and hunters from the late medieval period. Huntsmen in the book are described as wearing a *leine shrdill* or satin tunic – this may be a satin doublet or coat with a linen shirt underneath, a *cotin* or aketon, *luireach* or mail shirt and a *cinnbheirt* or bascinet. Each man is said to carry two *sleagha* or spears, a *sgiath* or shield, and a *lann*or or sword.[43]

The last Lord of the Isles, John of Islay, Earl of Ross (1434–1503), is described in the Books of Clanranald as wearing a well-fitting satin jerkin decorated with foreign birds on it. He had a fine mail shirt over which he wore a girdle 'brilliant with blue stones', and with a bronze clasp. He carried a 'long bladed sword', which was presumably a transitional West Highland claymore with an ivory hilt (probably walrus ivory) and wore gauntlets.

---

39 *RPS*, 1456/4. Date accessed: 2 October 2022.
40 *The Royal Commission on the Ancient and Historical Monuments of Scotland, Argyll. Volume 7 : Mid Argyll and Cowal: Medieval and Later Monuments* (Edinburgh, HMSO, 1992), p.90.
41 1494 TA I 240.
42 1513 TA IV 474.
43 A. E. M. Wiseman, *Chasing the Deer*, p.28.

WE CARRIED WAR-RAIMENT AND ARMS

His helmet was white or polished and jewelled. He also carried an axe of tempered steel.[44]

It is clear that not all men are wearing the huge saffron coloured linen shirts with a mantle draped over their shoulders, which was often fringed. This seems sometimes but not always to have been worn with bare legs and a short doublet over the shirt. Some men wore long hose cut on bias. Many men wore their hair long and loose about their shoulders with no hat. This aspects of their appearance was genuinely shocking to people from elsewhere who always (even in bed!) wore hats.

The hunting scene on the tomb to Alexander MacLeod, Lord of Dunvegan at St Clements, Rodel, Harris shows the clan chief and his men wearing armour as they would have for war. The chief is wearing a long aketon and mail shirt with a bascinet with an aventail carrying a claymore with a long handed axe in the other hand.[45] It's possible his clothing is exaggerated in length to show his status. The same style of armour is seen on figures carved on the tombs at Roscommon and Dungiven in Ireland as well as elsewhere in the West Highlands. It looks like he is wearing boots. Many men however wore shoes made from rawhide, called rillings, '*Thir rillingis ar ane kynde of schone rowch of raw vnbarkit leddir, quhare with Scottis (conforme to the ald fassoun of Romanis) vsit to pas in weris and hunting.*'[46] Macleod was present at the Battle of Bloody Bay [Blàr Bàgh na Fala] that took place either in 1481 or 1483 between John of Islay, Lord of the Isles and his son where MacLeod was either killed or he died subsequently at Dunvegan.

Macleod's attendants are both wearing fashionable, for the end of the 15th century, caps, which might possibly have been knitted and fulled, and fashionable short gowns. One attendant is wearing a long *leine* or shirt that comes down to over his knees and possibly some hose; the other is wearing long hose as in the Lowlands or England. They are both wearing buckled shoes. One man is carrying a crossbow and quiver. The contemporary historian, Hector Boece, describes Highlanders as 'carrying corsbowe, hand bowe, dart and slung.'[47] The other man is holding the leashes of his chief's dogs.[48]

This image is important in not only does it show a chieftain and his men ready for war, but it shows that they were aware of contemporary fashion elsewhere. A poem about the hunting down of the conspirators around James I's death in the early 15th century, quoted in the Book of Garth and

---

44   A. Cameron, M. A. Macbain, Rev. J. Kennedy (eds), The Book of Clanranald in *Reliquiae Celticae,* (Inverness, The Northern Counties Newspaper and Printing and Publishing Company, Limited, 1894), volume 2, pp.149–288 at pp.261–3.
45   J. W. M. Steer & K. A. Bannerman, *Late Medieval Monumental Sculpture*, p.98.
46   "Rilling n." *Dictionary of the Scots Language*. 2004. Scottish Language Dictionaries Ltd. Accessed 18 Sep 2021.
47   "Vangard n." *Dictionary of the Scots Language*. 2004. Scottish Language Dictionaries Ltd. Accessed 12 Oct 2022.
48   Ibid p.98. https://canmore.org.uk/collection/844032

Fortingall from the Dean of Lismore's collection, suggests that that they used 'the skins of wolves' for covering harps and possibly making bags.[49]

Martin Martin says:

> the first habit wore by persons of distinction in the Islands was the Leni-Croich, from the Irish word Leni which signifies a Shirt, Croich Saffron, because their shirts were dyed with that Herb; the ordinary number of ells to make this robe, was twenty four; as it was the Upper Garb, reaching below the knees; and tied with a belt around the middle.[50]

Saffron was extremely expensive at the time and, as Martin suggests in this passage, would therefore have only been used for the clothing of elite men.

The two-handed swords, such as that the Earl of Ross is described as having in the *Books of Clanranald*, were a 15th century innovation. Elite men in the West Highlands seem to have favoured the sword. The 'wild Scots of the Highlands and Islands' preferred bows and Jean de Froissart writes of the axes 'great axes, sharp and hard', being used the Scots who were 'well expert' in their use.[51] The type of axe that later became the better known Lochaber Axe – although there were several different types. John Major mentions, a small halbert carried by the 'wild Scots of the north' at the time of Bannockburn.[52] Martin says that the ancient (by which he means the 16th century, since that is for him in 1700 is just out of living memory):

> way of fighting was by set battles; and for Arms some had broad two-handed swords and head-pieces, and others Bows and Arrows. When all their arrows were spent, they attack'd one another with Sword in hand.[53]

In the early 16th century the use of the axe fell out of favour, to be replaced by the West Highland claymore and weapons similar to the 'Lochaber Axe', depending on social class.

---

49 D. Campbell, *The book of Garth and Fortingall : Historical Sketches Relating to the Districts of Garth, Fortingall, Athole, and Breadalbane.* (Inverness, The Northern Counties Newspaper and Printing Ltd, 1888).

50 M. Martin, *A Description of the Western Islands*, p.206.

51 D. H. Caldwell, 'Some Notes on Scottish Shafted Weapons', D. Caldwell, D (ed.), *Scottish Weapons and Fortifications* (Edinburgh, John Donald, 1981), p.256.

52 Although the description is contemporary to the writer in the early 16th century. D. H. Caldwell, 'Some Notes on Scottish shafted weapons', p.256.

53 M. Martin, *A Description of the Western Islands*, p.210.

There is a medieval seal of Orkney produced for Norway a few years before Orkney became Scottish in 1472, where the two men are shown in clothing worn by the medieval Orcardians, and their clothes show some influences from mainland Scotland. The dress that these two supporters are wearing presumably represents the formal outfit of a wealthy Orcadian. It appears that they are wearing a belted knee length tunic with decoration possibly embroidery at the cuffs, hose and then *rivlins*, the long soft boots that Highlanders also wore at this period. Although bare headed one of them appears to be wearing a hood.

Martin mentions the bow, and although there not many depictions of Highlanders using bows, Highlanders provided many of the archers in the Royal armies. There are however a few images of archers. For example, there is the huntsman at Rodel who has a crossbow and a hunter in the act of killing a deer on a grave slab at St Maelrubba's Church, Arisaig from the 15th century.[54] The Gaelic for a bow (*bogha*) derives from the old Norse. The 15th century feud between the Mackays and the Mathiesons was settled by Iver Mathieson killing the victorious Mackay chief, Angus Dubh with an arrow.[55] The Battle of the Arrow at Eilean Donan Castle in 1539 was decided by a single arrow shot by the Constable of the castle when Duncan Macrae killed Donald Gorm MacDonald, Lord of Sleat, as his men were about to get into the castle. The barbed arrow wounded Sleat fatally after hitting him in the knee.[56] Pitscottie says that MacLean of Duart was on the Flodden campaign in 1513 with a force of 600 men armed with bows and half langs and clad in habergeons, and his somewhat exaggerated description of the battle of Sauchieburn in 1488 says that James III had a vanguard of 10,000 Highlanders armed with bows, under the Earls of Huntly and Atholl.[57]

The West Highland men under the Earl of Argyll that turned out for the battle of Pinkie in 1547 were described as four thousand Irish [Gaelic speaking West Highlanders] archers[58]. At least some of these would have been Clann Domhnaill (Clan Donald South) and Macleans.

Scottish bows were considerably cheaper than English ones:

> ane dosane of hand bowis, send at the Kingis grace command to James Canoth, of the quhiikis the tane half was Scottis bowis and the tother half Inglis, price of the pece of the Inglis bowis xvj S. [sixteen shillings], and price of the pece of the Scotis bowis ix [nine shillings].

---

54 D. H. Caldwell, 'Having the Right Kit: West Highlanders', p.162.
55 A. Mackay, *The Book of the Mackays*, (Edinburgh, N. MacLeod, 1906), p.58.
56 C. Peers, *The Highland Battles: Warfare on Scotland's Northern Frontier in the Early Middle Ages*, (Barnsley, Pen and Sword, 2020) p.34.
57 D. H. Caldwell, 'How Well Prepared was James IV to Fight by Land and Sea in 1513?' *Journal of the Sydney Society for Scottish History 14*, (Sydney 2013), p.38.
58 R. Lindsay of Piscottie (E. J. G. Mackay, ed.), *The Historie and Chronicles of Scotland*, (Edinburgh, Scottish Text Society, 1899–1911), p.110.

Scottish bows were more readily available and perhaps shorter. However, a description of the supporters of Donald Dubh, the last credible claimant to the Lordship of the Isles says that they were 'very tall men, armed mostly in mail with long swords and long bows.'[59]

---

59   D. G. White, 'Henry VIII's Irish Kerne in France and Scotland, *Irish Sword*, iii 1957–8, pp.213–25, quoted at p.222.

4

Birlinns, ships and galleys

> The brown-sailed barques are furnished
> With swords of ivory and gold;
> Alongside a rank of bright spear-points[1]

The likelihood of a Viking era origin for the West Highland galley, or *birlinn* (a *birling* in Scots) is extremely strong as can be seen from the early 14th century poem quoted at the beginning of this chapter.[2] Galleys were used in pursuit of inter-clan warfare during the *Linn nan Creach* or 'Age of Forays'. Starting in the 13th century and continuing up to the 15th century, large numbers of heavily armed warriors were transported by galleys to fight in Ireland. Similarly, during the 16th century galleys carried 'redshank' mercenaries to fight in Ireland. A law of 1430 required all barons and lords living on or near the west coast to maintain galleys.[3] Although they seem to be an exclusively West Highland phenomenon by the early modern period that does not look to have been the case in the medieval Scotland, there is a representation of a galley on a 15th century seal of Renfrew, which now lies about six miles (9.7 kilometres) to the west of Glasgow in the western central Lowlands.[4]

---

1   W. McLeod & M. Bateman (eds), *Duanaire Na Sracaire: Songbook of the Pillagers Anthology of Scotland's Gaelic Verse to 1600* (Edinburgh, Origin, 2019) – Dal Chabhlaighar Chaisteal Suibhne (A Meeting of a Fleet Against the Castle of Suibne) p.223.
2   West Highland in this instance is taken to include all of the Hebrides and mainland Argyllshire. Dr D. C. McWhannell, 'Campbell of Breadalbane and Campbell of Argyll Boatbuilding Accounts 1600 to 1700, *The Mariner's Mirror*, 89:4, 2003, pp.405–424. D. Caldwell, 'Having the Right Kit: West Highlanders fighting in Ireland'. S. Duffy (ed.), *The World of the Galloglass: Kings, Warlords and Warriors in Ireland and Scotland 1200–1600* (Dublin, Four Courts Press, 2007, 2016), p.145.
3   RPS, 1430/21, accessed September 2022,
4   Caldwell, 'Having the Right Kit…', p.145.

The galleys were clinker built – meaning that the overlapping planks were joined with pins or nails – open hulled boats. The closest modern survival in Scotland is probably the Orcadian yawl. They had a single central sail, which could be either linen or wool. Linen was produced in Scotland and was therefore likely to have been used for sails. A woollen sail was implied in the order for 'plaiding' for the sail of a MacLeod birlinn in 1706, and woollen sails were still being used in the Gairloch area in the nineteenth century while part of a rental for Tiree in 1622 required the provision of a 'saill and hair taickle to a galley'.[5] This was perhaps part of the Norse heritage since the Vikings had used woollen sails on their ships.[6] Sails were often patterned or coloured and were likely to have carried personal symbols, much like on a battlefield to aid identification.

On the carving of a 16th century galley that appears on the tomb of Alexander MacLeod at St Clement's Church, Rodel, Harris the sail of the galley appears to be made up from small rectangular panels of cloth arranged joined horizontally at the edges with tape.[7] This galley was a very large one for the time at 34 oars.[8] An early representation of a galley is shown on the seal of Aonghus Mor Mac Domhnaill of Islay. This 13rd century image is particularly interesting since it shows a rudder at the stern.[9]

The King also had a red and blue standard made for his ship so this was not unique to the galleys. The King's standard was twelve ells long [just over eleven metres]. It had a saltire on the blue section beside the pole, 'to pant a St Androis cors', then the royal lion and unicorn. It is possible that it also had thistles embroidered on it, or a motto but that's unclear from the Treasurer's accounts.[10] Ensigns and standards like these, can be seen on many galley carvings and appear to be of a similar size of that of the King. Like his standard, the galley standards were there in order to show the presence of the lord who owned the boat, while trumpets may have been used for signalling.[11]

The West Highland galley was key to the exercise of lordly power on the Western seaboard and the maintenance of a society dominated by a warrior aristocracy. The Lords of the Isles used a galley as their heraldic device in

---

5   D. Rixson, *The West Highland Galley*, (Edinburgh, Birlinn, 1998), p.22.
6   B. Cooke, C. Christiansen & L. Hammarlund, 'Viking Woollen Square-Sails and Fabric Cover Factor', *International Journal of Nautical Archaeology*. 31. (Taylor & Francis, 2002) pp.202–210.
7   Dr D. C. McWhannell, 'The Galleys of Argyll', *The Mariner's Mirror*, 88:1, 2002, p.18.
8   D. Rixson, *The West Highland Galley*, p.45. It is likely that earlier galleys were larger and that they gradually got smaller over time because of the different demands being put on them.
9   D. Caldwell, 'Having the Right Kit…', p.144.
10 1512 TA IV 477, Hodge, Edinburgh Castle Research, p.198.
11 The King of Scots certainly used trumpeters, for example. 'Iij Scottis trumpatis play and at the outputting of the Kingis grets chipe'. 1511 TA IV 312.

BIRLINNS, SHIPS AND GALLEYS

various forms.[12] Galleys were used for personal transport, for pillage, as troop transports, and for trading, 'Scots in your smooth ship, to plunder the sea.'[13] In 1595, Captain George Thornton said, 'the Scottish gallies of great swiftness by oars, hardly to be followed for good service by Her Majesty's pinnaces.'[14] The galleys were not much use as fighting ships by this period, however, since they couldn't carry artillery nonetheless they could move quickly through the seas carrying men and plunder. In 1589, a Scottish force took the hides and tallow of over 1,000 cattle when they sailed from Erris in Mayo; they had about 600 men in seven galleys, meaning there was approximately 85 men in each galley.[15]

The total cost of the birlinn in 1635, including a sail and plus running costs, probably represented around a third of the net annual income from Campbell of Glenorchy's lands in Argyllshire. Although clearly Glenorchy had further sources of income, it was nonetheless a significant investment.[16] Their relatively small size made them ideal for the lochs, beaches, and small inlets up and down the coast, which were used as harbours and safe anchorages. A 16th century source for these is Alexander Lindsay's *A Rutter for the Scottish Seas*, an early navigational guide. This is the oldest Scottish 'rutter' (an early 16th century term for a set of sailing directions, a word derived from the French *routier*) prepared for James V's voyage to the Western Isles. Lindsay was probably the pilot on this voyage. Moving southwards from Cape Wrath, on the very northwest of Scotland he lists the beaches, lochs and other anchorages down the west coast, such as Gairloch, the Inner Sound between Ramsay and Applecross, the sheltered water between the Crowlin Island in the Inner Hebrides; the Duart Bays in the Sound of Mull, Tobermory Bay; Tarbert on Jura, and the Sound of Islay. The list ends with Lamlash Bay,

Detail from the tomb of Alexander Macleod c.1528, showing a highland galley or birlin (© RCAHMS)

---

12 A. Campbell of Airds, 'West Highland Heraldry and The Lordship of the Isles', *The Lordship of the Isles*, R, Oram (ed.) (Leiden, Brill, 2014) pp.200–10.

13 F. Cannan, *Galloglass 1250–1600: Gaelic Mercenary Warrior*, (Oxford, Osprey, 2010) quoted on p.13.

14 Quoted in D. Rixson, *The West Highland Galley*, p.34.

15 Caldwell, 'Having the Right Kit…', p.147.

16 Dr D. C. McWhannell, *Campbell of Breadalbane and Campbell of Argyll Boatbuilding Accounts 1600 to 1700*, p.409.

protected by the Holy Island on the east side of Arran, and Loch Ranza on the north.[17]

The Earl of Argyll, who had a large number of galleys available to him, was able to move his men up and down the Western seaboard with impunity. In 1560, he offered the English government 3,000 men, which was twice the size of the English army in Ireland at the time.[18] Men could be landed on beaches throughout the West Highlands and Islands, on the Irish coast, and on the coasts of Ayrshire and Galloway. In order for this to be feasible, keepers of small castles throughout his lands were expected to have ready a galley or birlin. In September 1573, the Earl outlined that Donnchadh Campbell MacIver, captain of Inveraray and baillie of Glenara:

> must ... keep and maintain a small birling or galley of 16 oars in our earldom with the rest of our ships, just as the Bailies of Glenara have been accustomed to do in past times for us and our predecessors.[19]

The Auchinleck Chronicle suggests that Donald Balloch, Chief of Clan Donald South, on a raid in 1452 had a hundred galleys with 5,000 to 6,000 men – suggesting that each galley was taking 50 to 60 men and had 16 to 20 oars.[20]

The last uprising that realistically attempted to restore the Lordship of the Isles was led by Donald Dubh, in 1544/5, which received widespread support from clans within the Western Isles, including the MacDonalds of Clanranald, the MacLeods of Lewis, the MacLeods of Harris, and the MacLeans of Duart. Dubh planned to muster 4,100 and 180 galleys.[21]

At the start of 17th century, this is the Scottish Crown's view of what a galley was:

> Ane galley is ane veshel of xviij airis and abone to xxiiij airis: ane birling is ane veshell of xij airis and abone to xviij airis. The birth of ane galley and birling and the number of men of weir quhilk they ar able to carye is estimat according to the number of their airis, compting three men to every air.
> [A galley is a vessel of eighteen oars and above to twenty-four oars: a birling is a vessel of twelve oars and above to eighteen oars. The

---

17 S. Murdoch, *The Terror of the Seas? : Scottish Maritime Warfare, 1513–1713*. (Boston, Brill, 2010), p.36.
18 J. Dawson, 'The Fifth Earl of Argyle, Gaelic Lordship and Political Power in Sixteenth-Century Scotland', *The Scottish Historical Review*, volume 67, no. 183, 1988, pp.1–27 at p.3.
19 R. M. Crawford, *Warfare in the West Highlands and Isles of Scotland*, quoted on p.88.
20 D. H. Caldwell, *Islay: The Land of the Lordship*, (Edinburgh, Birlinn, 2008), p.67.
21 A. Cathcart, 'The Forgotten '45: Donald Dubh's Rebellion in Archipelagic Context', *The Scottish Historical Review*, volume 91, no. 232, 2012, pp.239–264.

berth of a galley and birling and the number of men which they are able to carry is estimated according to the number of their oars counting three men to every oar].[22]

This is not intended to mean that that three men were required to pull every oar, merely that this is amount of space that there would be per oar.

In 1435, a large barge was built in Leith for the Royal fleet.[23] In 1437, James I's fleet consisted of a great ship, two other ships, the barge and a balinger (a small sea going ship). It is possible that James I, who is known to have encouraged shipbuilding, had hired men from the Netherlands to assist in constructing his own vessels. During James I's reign, shipbuilding also took place on the West coast at Ayr, Dumbarton and Glasgow.

Merchant ships with French assistance were needed to bolster the small Scots navy.[24] James had attempted to legislate to control them:

it is decreed that all barons and lords having lands and lordships near the sea in the west and in the northern regions, and namely beside the isles, that they have galleys…And that the said galleys be made and repaired by May come twelve months under the pain of half a merk to be raised to the king's use from each oar.

This was not really a success,[25] and James needed to do something more since Scottish merchant ships were coming under attack and the Scots crown had no way of defending them. Additionally, the English fleet was able to sail into Leith without encountering any resistance in 1482 in support of Albany and the Duke of Gloucester's ultimately unsuccessful campaign because of Scotland's weakness at sea.[26] It was, however, this campaign during which Berwick fell into English hands for the final time. Therefore James began a programme of shipbuilding.

Other European monarchs were beginning to arm the new big three-masted sailing ships with increasingly heavy and effective artillery. Pitscottie writes of a sea fight in 1490 between the Scottish sea captain Andrew Wood commanding the *Yellow Carvel* and the *Flower* and the English captain, Stephen Bull, with three ships. The fight involved artillery and crossbows.[27] Thus, the combination of attacks on shipping plus the difficulties of defending the vulnerable coast without a navy of any sort drove the King

---

22 Dr D. C. McWhannell, 'The Galleys of Argyll', p.14.
23 MacDonald, A, The Kingdom of Scotland at War: 1332–1488, in A Military History of Scotland eds E. J. Spiers, Crang & M. J. Strickland (Edinburgh, Edinburgh University Press, 2012, 2014) pp158–181 at p171
24 A. MacDonald, *The Kingdom of Scotland at War: 1332–1488*, p.171.
25 RPS 1430/21.
26 N. Macdougall, *James IV*, (Edinburgh, John Donald, 1997), p.225.
27 R. Lindsay of Piscottie, *The Historie and Chronicles of Scotland*, E. J. G Mackay (ed.), (Edinburgh, Scottish Text Society, 1899–1911) p.226–8.

into building ships. Over the winter of 1494–5, the royal accounts show the start of a shipbuilding programme.

The following summer James mounted an expedition to the west coast of Scotland, leaving from Dumbarton in July 1494, and again in the May after, going via the Clyde to Bute and then to Kintyre and finally anchoring off Mingary Castle in Ardnamurchan.[28] In 1502 he sent a small fleet of ships to Scandinavia to aid King Hans of Denmark against his rebels. This fleet was probably mostly hired ships: the *Towaich*, the *Douglas*, the *Christopher*, and perhaps the *Jacat* and the *Trinity*.[29]

A barge costing £500 Scots was built for King James, at Dumbarton. '1494 [no date], To the byggin of the king's rowbarges by-gite in Dunbartane, the tymmyre fra Loch Lowmond and divers uthir woddis.' A ship was purchased from the Laird of Laucht, repaired and equipped, in Dumbarton, and James ordered several "row barges" to be built. The subsequent expedition included an important development in the use of artillery in Scotland as firing large guns from the decks or gun-ports of ships was recorded for the first time at the siege of Cairnburgh Castle, in the Treshnish Islands off Mull, by James in 1504. His force besieged the Macleans for several weeks, the ships were supplied with guns under the command of Hans, one of the royal gunners.[30] The guns must have been fired from the ships since there is no suitable landing site near the castle.[31] Cutting gun-ports in ships' hulls is supposedly a French innovation from 1501.[32]

Sailors in the 16th century often wore thrummed hats, 'For thromes viii s', Skipper Henry Morton was buying them in the 1580s. These hats were frequently worn by working class men and occasionally women of the same lower class. The felt on the hat was worked with the short end of the wool pulled through giving it a shaggy appearance. The jack of plates was a popular piece of armour on board ship since it allowed movement and gave protection. As with their contemporaries elsewhere, sailors dressed according to their station in life. Therefore, the skippers and captains customarily dressed as gentlemen. If the ship carried a barber surgeon then he would wear a learned man's coif, probably of satin, underneath his knitted hat[33]. Slops (loose full-length, trouser-like hose) are possible wear

---

28   J. Irving, *The Book of Dumbartonshire: A History of the County, Burghs, Parishes, and Lands, Memoirs of Families, and Notices of Industries Carried on in the Lennox District*, (Edinburgh, 1879), p.129.
29   N. Macdougall, *James IV*, (Edinburgh, John Donald, 1997), p.231.
30   N. Macdougall, *James IV*, (Edinburgh, John Donald, 1997), pp.185–186. 1513 TA IV 502
31   D. Caldwell, 'Edinburgh Castle as a Gunhouse', p.26.
32   D. H. Caldwell, 'James IV at Land and Sea', p.57.
33   There was a velvet and satin coif found on Mary Rose, dated to 1545, which probably belonged to the barber surgeon. There was also a barber surgeon at Pinkie unfortunately, no one recorded his clothes. J. Malcolm-Davies & N. Mikhalia, *The Typical Tudor: Reconstructing Everyday 16th Century Dress*, (Lightwater, Fat Goose Press, 2022) p.172.

for working class sailors in the 16th century, although most would have worn tight long hose or breeches. It is likely that they went bare foot on board ship.

James had a camp bed, a *letacampbed* (from the French, lit de camp). This was a bed that could be dismantled and packed into a box – there is an entry in the 1520s for coffers or boxes for the beds. The mattress was suspended on ropes. 'Gevin for the making of ane harnes to turs the Kingis letacampbed.'[34] This bed was also sometimes termed a tursing bed, 'iij boltis of fustiane, to be fustiannis to his tursing bed.'[35]

Guns, ammunition, rope and cable were imported from Flanders, while timber, tools and nails were brought from France.[36] James IV established royal garrisons and fortifications around the coast, at Kilkerran Castle near Campbeltown, Tarbert at the mouth of the Clyde, Dunaverty Castle, Kintyre, and Ailsa Craig as he began to develop his navy.[37] Shipbuilders were brought to Leith from Brittany, France and the Netherlands.

A shipwright called 'Goherrall', possibly from Portugal, is recorded as building a ship at Dumbarton around 1506. Timber for the Leith shipyards was brought from forests in the Borders, Fife, Badenoch and Lochaber. Keels for the large ships were imported from France. The *Margaret*, launched in 1505, cost around 8,000 pounds Scots. When the *Margaret* was launched an hundred casks were lashed to the hull to help her float high enough to clear the sands, since Leith is a tidal port. The cost of the ship was greater than a quarter of James IV's annual income at that time. She had three masts and was armed with artillery, including one large gun and several smaller pieces, and crossbows. When she sailed with the rest of the fleet in 1513, she had a crew of an hundred men and five gunners.[38]

In 1504, James bought a small ship from a Breton merchant, Michael Denis. It must have been relatively small as it cost only £100. Soon after he also bought another ship, the *Treasurer*.[39] In 1505, the *Columb*, a French barque was sent from Dumbarton with the royal gunner, Robert Herwort, on board to ensure the surrender of Brodick Castle, which had been seized by Walter Stewart:[40]

> To Hans, gunner, for the expenses for bringing artillery (four falcons and ane cannon) forth of the castle, 9s 4d; to a wright two days, 2s 8d; for carrying of those five guns to the ship, 20s; for carrying down

---

34 1495 TA I 238.
35 1495 Ib 239.
36 Dr D. C. McWhannell, 'Campbell of Breadalbane and Campbell of Argyll Boatbuilding Accounts', p.410.
37 N. Macdougall, *James IV*, pp.104–5 & 115–16.
38 1502 TA II 281, 282 Ib III 90, 142; Ib IV. 505–507.
39 1506 TA II 445.
40 N. Macdougall, *James IV*, p.234.

to the ship two barrels powder, 16d; … 8d; for two powder bags, two iron plates for chargers, 4s.[41]

The *Margaret* had previously been armed from Edinburgh Castle arsenal on 25 May 1505, but this time, instead of a traditional wrought iron bombard, the main armament was a heavy bronze cannon, firing an iron roundshot of around 36 pounds (16.3 kilograms). The ship and this large gun, along with the above guns, were probably being deployed for the naval campaign on 19 June 1506. Later in June Hans was also paid for returning the guns and mending their carriages. Additionally James hired ships for his campaigns from the Leith skipper, Robert Barton, who later commanded the *Michael*, his brothers and others, as well as buying additional ships, including the *Unicorn*, from France, in 1506.[42]

James seems to have had four large ships at his disposal – the *Michael*, for at least a short period, the *Margaret*, the *Treasurer* and the *James* – additionally, there were also three smaller ships. James also periodically hired ships from the Bartons – John Barton and his three sons, Robert, John and Andrew. MacDougall says that it was they and their ships that 'gave the Scots their European reputation as formidable opponents at sea, and as pirates.'[43]

The *Michael* took five years to build, was launched in 1511 and cost approximately 30,000 pounds, an amount roughly equal to the King's entire annual income.[44] The artillery cost more in addition, 'Hir artaillze quhilk was werie [very] great and costlie to the king.'[45] Men such as Jacques (Jacat in the Scots records) Terrel who was paid £10, from France, oversaw the building of the great *Michael*, while Jennan Diew from Brittany and John Lorans from Dieppe appear in the records of Leith. The 'great scheip' *Michael* used wood from Fife, from Darnaway Forest in Moray. The ship *Raven* brought timber at a cost of 14 pounds from Moray, Lanarkshire, Cawdor, France, Denmark and Norway.[46] Pittscottie says that the Great *Michael* had six cannon on every side, with three great basselis (basilisks) and smaller artillery, 'mayan [moyen] and batterit facouns and quarter fallcouns, (bastard and quarter Falcons), hagbutts and cullvering; and doubill doggis (dog guns). The ship was also equipped with crossbows and handbows.[47]

Lindsay gives the *Michael*'s dimensions as 240 feet (73 m) long and 35 ft (11 metres) in beam. This was a genuinely large ship if the dimensions

---

41 1506 TA II 203.
42 D. H. Caldwell, *James IV at Land and Sea*, p.51.
43 N. Macdougall, *James IV*, p.238.
44 Dr D. C. McWhannell, 'Campbell of Breadalbane and Campbell of Argyll Boatbuilding Accounts,' p.412.
45 Piscottie, *Historie* I, p.251.
46 Ib, p.412.
47 Piscottie, *Historie* I, p.251.

given by Pitscottie are to be believed, although it is quite possible that he exaggerated its size. The 'skipper', Alexander Routh of Michael, was paid £7 per month.[48] John Barton, the Commander received £5 12s for himself and a man.[49] Pitscottie says that the *Michael* had three hundred sailors, as well as six score (120) gunners and a thousand men-of-war (although it is worth mentioning that there is no evidence that the *Michael* had additional soldiers as well as her sailors), besides her captains, skippers, and quartermasters.[50]

The accounts give the names and pay of 40 mariners that were on the *Margaret* and 30 that were on the *James* however supplies imply that there were far more sailors on both.[51] The King also had a smaller ship, a bark 'callit the Gabriel' built.[52] The small *Gabriel* was manned by Frenchmen, having 10 men and a boy, and was commanded by one, Perynot.[53]

In June 1512, the ship *Lark* was docked at Airth near Falkirk on the banks of the Forth and the barque *James*, which had been purchased for £65, had a new mast put in her the following month there.[54]

Three great guns, 'iii greit gunnys', were brought down from the castle to the ships at Leith, each needed six carts to move it, at a cost of 2s per cart, totalling £1 16*s*.[55] In May of that year a 'galay' was being built in Glasgow. The next year, the accounts record that nine shillings four pence was spent on red lead and linseed oil for colouring the three great iron guns that were put into the great ship (the *Michael*).[56]

By 1513 the Scottish fleet consisted of some 38 ships either built in Scotland, given to the Crown, or captured, 15 of these could be considered warships. These included four main vessels – the *Michael*, the *Margaret*, the *Treasurer* and the *James*. The fleet was commanded by the Earl of Arran and comprised the *Michael*, the *Margaret* and the *James*, and the other eight ships. The *Bark of Abbeyfield* and the Spanish bark were royal vessels; the rest were hired. This fleet was sent to France in 1513 to prepare for a combined attack on England.[57] This projected attack didn't happen and while the other three ships returned to Scotland, the *Michael* was sold to France at approximately half what it cost to build her.[58] In June 1515, the remaining warships, the *Margaret* and the *James*, arrived at Dumbarton and

---

48 1513 TA IV 503, 4.
49 Piscottie, *Historie* I, p.505.
50 Piscottie, *Historie* I, p.251. There were, however, another 45 men, three pilots and two gunners from the French crown for the *Michael*. 1513 TA IV 487.
51 D. H. Caldwell, 'James IV at Land and Sea' p.59. The *Margaret* had about 284 men, and the *James* about 248 men.
52 1512 TA IV 453.
53 Ib 453.
54 1511 TA IV 280, 281.
55 1512 TA IV 451.
56 1513 TA IV 509.
57 S. Murdoch, *The Terror of the Seas? : Scottish Maritime Warfare, 1513–1713.* (Boston, Brill, 2010), p.34.
58 S. Murdoch, *The Terror of the Seas? : Scottish Maritime Warfare, 1513–1713.* (Boston, Brill, 2010), p.35.

the fourteen guns on board, including two heavy cannons, were taken by boat to Glasgow.[59]

By the 1530s, the Scots fleet had recovered enough for its ships to be patrolling the seas between France and Scotland. In early 1531, James was ready for a new expedition to the Isles and wrote to the King of France, François I, of his intentions to blow the Islesmen out of their ships and castles with his 'culverin' - clearly this expedition was not intended to win hearts and minds.[60] It is likely that the 'culverin' that James was writing about is the bronze gun outside Inverary Castle, which is sometimes attributed to a shipwreck after the Spanish Armada a half-century later.

In 1536, James left Scotland for France with his new navy including some of the captured ships. He sailed on the *Mary Willoughby* which had been taken by Hector Maclean (Eachann Mór Maclean) and Alexander MacIan of Dunyvaig on a raid on the Isle of Man with his galleys and subsequently given to the King.[61] Pittcottie suggests that the *Lion* went as well.[62] The skipper of the *Mary Willoughby* was Hans Anderson.[63]

The ships that sailed to collect Mary of Guise were the *Salamander*, the *Moriset*, the *Mary Willoughby* and what was called 'a French challop'.[64] At this point, the Scottish navy had three ships of any size: the *Mary Willoughby*, the *Unicorn* and the *Salamander*. In 1540, for his expedition to the Western Isles James' fleet of six ships had as its flagship the *Salamander*, which had been a gift from the King of France, probably with the great bombard *Mons Meg*, on board.[65]

James was also building ships, or rather galleys, of his own.[66] By building galleys, James was making a statement about himself as a Renaissance Prince since the galley was the iconic warship of the era. An irony since, of course, Scotland already had a galley building culture but these new ships were different because these were inspired by the rediscovered ideals of the Renaissance (or at least that century's renaissance) and they could carry guns which birlins couldn't. It is likely that the artillery fortification called 'the Spur' at Edinburgh Castle was designed to echo a galley.[67]

After James' death the Royal flagship, the *Lion* carried a battery of guns, probably including at least two cannons and perhaps as many as four. She

---

59 1515 TA V 16,17, 18, 38.
60 J. Cameron, *James V: the Personal Rule, 1528–1542*, (Edinburgh, Tuckwell Press, 1998), p.136.
61 S. Murdoch, *The Terror of the Seas?* p.40. D. H. Caldwell, *Islay*, p.81.
62 Pittscottie, *Historie*, I 367.
63 1539 TA VII 190.
64 A. Thomas, *Princelie Majestie: The Court of James V of Scotland, 1528–1542* (Edinburgh, John Donald, 2005), p.158–9.
65 'Postscript Mons Meg's original Carriage and the Carvings of Artillery in Edinburgh Castle' in D. H. Caldwell (ed.), *Scottish Weapons & Fortifications 1100–1800* (Edinburgh: John Donald, 1981), pp.437–441.
66 A. Thomas, *Princelie Majestie*, p.159.
67 A. Hodge, *Edinburgh Castle : The Medieval Documents*, p.511.

cruised as a heavy commerce raider until 1547, when she was ambushed by the English while on a diplomatic mission.[68]

---

[68] A. Hodge, *Edinburgh Castle : The Medieval Documents*, p.512.

5

The Field of Flodden

> King James the fourt was slaine in the feild of Flowdane be our auld inymies of Ingland. Thair was in this field mony of the Scottis nobillis slane.[1]

In the years before the battle of Flodden in 1513, James IV had been building up the capacity of Scotland to deliver a well-armed, capable army. In 1502–4 he made payments to Passing, 'armorar ... for the setting up of a 'harness myln', this being the workshop of an armourer.[2] 'To the Frauch armorar to set up his harnas myln.'[3]

James IV also had armour bought for him before his marriage.[4] The King had a jacket and breeches of fine 'Milan' fustian made for wearing with armour.[5] In 1512, the king had a bevor delivered to him from John Forman.[6] English sources record that the army was well equipped with armour and the *Treasurer's Accounts* show that munition armour was bought in large quantities. For example, as late as July 1513, 12 carts full of armour [*harness*] were brought from Denmark and in the last part of their journey carried from Newhaven to Edinburgh Castle.[7]

After the battle, William Tour, an English armourer, had 350 sallets, gorgets, backs, breasts and pairs of splints for sale, which gives an indication

---

1　T. Thomson (ed.), *Diurnal of the remarkable occurents that have passed within the country of Scotland since the death of James the Fourth till the year MDLXXV (1575)*, (Edinburgh, Bannatyre Club, 1833), p.3.
2　C. A. Whitelaw, S. Baxter (eds), *Scottish Arms Makers...* p.60.
3　1502 TA II 143.
4　1502/3 TA II 359.
5　1508/9 TA IV 23.
6　1512 TA IV 205. John Forman was probably a merchant rather than an armourer since the king also had a schapioun delivered which implies the bevor may well have been imported and not made locally.
7　1508 IV 114, 1513 IV 419.

of the amount of armour there must have been at the battle.[8] The men who led the columns at Flodden were all chosen men with 'speres on foot… the most assured harnessed that hath bene sene.'[9] The army at Flodden fought on foot with long spears, or pikes and Dr Caldwell suggests that this may be directly linked to the Scots' experience of Sauchieburn.[10]

Ordinary men at Flodden for the most part wore their own clothes with a jack over the top. The lower class men's hose was made from fabrics like frieze or kersey, which was a popular choice due to its stretching when cut on the bias. 'Ane pair red and blew carsay hois'[11] and doublets from fustian. As with separate hose of the early part of the previous century, they could end at the ankle, have a fabric stirrup under the foot or be footed. In the case of the latter these could be made with a woollen or leather sole. The king had a jak 'lynt with fustian', made by Thomas Edgar and his children.[12]

Many men wore coats made from russet, which with its natural colour was often associated with the rural working class.[13] Their bonnets were, for the most part, knitted and fulled, there had been a bonnet makers' guild in Dundee since 1494. Many were blue but the blue bonnet had not yet become ubiquitous for the Scots and red or black for those of the middling sort were equally likely. The brims were normally either a single circle or divided in two usually knitted with the crown. Quite a few detached single or double ear flaps survive, suggesting that these were often made separately and sewn in place. Three years before Flodden, Aberdeen shoemakers were told to sell single soled men's shoes for thirteen or fourteen pence and double soled shoes for two shillings. Controlling the price suggests that most men expected to wear shoes.[14] A lot of men wore a simple knapscull and the Aberdeen records record the men 'with jak and knapscall, Dense aix or halbart'.[15] Although in 1508, William Dagleish, a lorimer was paid for 'thre lokkis to basnetis' and 'tua claspes to ane basnet'.[16]

Those men who had armour, continued to wear coat armour, this might be their own coat of Arms (this was personal to them and was not worn by their adherents) or possibly a livery coat. These were often quartered in the livery colours. The Royal Household did not have livery colours. The King had the royal lion put on his coat armour, 'vij day of August, for iij elnis

---

8 D. H. Caldwell, 'How Well Prepared was James IV to Fight by Land and Sea', p.38.
9 G. Phillips, *Scotland in the Age of Military Revolution, 1488–1560*, p.184.
10 D. H. Caldwell, 'How Well Prepared was James IV to Fight by Land and Sea', p.39.
11 1511 TA IV 262.
12 1507 TA III 263, 414. The children were paid 8 shillings. Thomas Edgar was a tailor like many who made jaks since it involved cutting linen rather than making armour.
13 For a longer discussion of materials see J. Malcolm-Davies & N. Mikhalia, *The Typical Tudor*, p.30.
14 E. Gemmill, *Debt, Distraint, Display and Dead Men's Treasure*, p.367.
15 J. Stuart, (ed.), *Extracts from the Council Register of the Burgh of Aberdeen, 1398–1625* Volume 1 (Aberdeen, Spalding Club, 1844–8), p.130.
16 1508 TA III 397

crammesy satyne to be lyonis to the Kingis cote armour; ilk elne iiij vj unce silk to the said coit-armour.'[17] It is possible that some of the men of the Royal Household may also have had the red lion of Scotland like the king since this was more than the King's personal heraldic badge.

An act of Parliament in 1471 had required all imported and locally made spears to be at least six ells long (approximately 5.6 metres). Ten years later, this was changed to a length of at least five and a half ells (5.17 metres) or five ells before the burr. An English spy's report in February 1512/13, concerning the Scottish preparations for war, says that there were considerable amounts of what he calls 'lance staves' in Edinburgh Castle.[18] Contemporary English chronicler, Edward Hall, writing 30 years later in 1548 said that in 1513, the Scots were importing daily from Veere (known in Scotland as Campevere) in the Netherlands, long spears called 'colleyne clowystes'.[19]

King Louis XII of France sent a small contingent of French military experts to help command the pikemen on the field of battle. These experts were led by the Sieur D'Aussi and included 50 men-at-arms and 40 captains.[20]

A number of minstrels and trumpeters, to whom payments are recorded in the Treasurer's Accounts, gave signals and encouraged the army on the march. On the field the King and his commanders made good use of his musicians, at least some of whom were Italian and French, and who had recently been given clothing, 'goune, doublattis and hois.' The hose were likely to have been black as were the doublets that laced to the long hose and the gown was probably either tawny or brown:[21]

> The king gart blaw the trumpitis and sett his men in order of battell. Then the trumpitis blew on everie sycle and the wangairdis [vanguard] ioyn itt togither. Then the Earle of Huntlie and lord Home blew their trumpattis and convenitt thair men agane to their standartis. ...The Earle of Huntlie ... callit his men togither be sloghorne [battle-cry] and sound of trumpit to haue passit to the king.[22]

---

17 1513 TA IV 413.
18 D. H. Caldwell, 'How Well Prepared was James IV to Fight by Land and Sea', p.41.
19 D. H. Caldwell, 'How Well Prepared was James IV to Fight by Land and Sea', p.42. Campevere was the staple right for Scotland, from the Dutch *stapelrecht*, and was a medieval right accorded to certain ports – the staple ports. It required merchant ships to unload their goods at the port and to display them for sale for a certain period, often three days. Only after that option had been given to locals were traders allowed to reload their cargo and go on with the remaining unsold goods.
20 1513 TA 515
21 1512 TA IV 430. It's not clear why they were importing these particular spears from Cologne. Clowystes means nails so it's a joke of sorts.
22 Pitscottie, *History*, volume i, pp.269–72.

A. 15th century knight
(Illustration by Seán Ó Brógain © Helion & Company 2023)
See Colour Plate Commentaries for further information.

B. Galloglass/Chief
(Illustration by Seán Ó Brógain © Helion & Company 2023)
See Colour Plate Commentaries for further information.

C. Soldier at Pinkie
(Illustration by Seán Ó Brógain © Helion & Company 2023)
See Colour Plate Commentaries for further information.

D. Borderer
(Illustration by Seán Ó Brógain © Helion & Company 2023)
See Colour Plate Commentaries for further information.

E. Marian Gunner
(Illustration by Seán Ó Brógain © Helion & Company 2023)
See Colour Plate Commentaries for further information.

F. Highland Gentleman
(Illustration by Seán Ó Brógain © Helion & Company 2023)
See Colour Plate Commentaries for further information.

G. Highland Archer
(Illustration by Seán Ó Brógain © Helion & Company 2023)
See Colour Plate Commentaries for further information.

H. Later Highlander
(Illustration by Seán Ó Brógain © Helion & Company 2023)
See Colour Plate Commentaries for further information.

THE FIELD OF FLODDEN

In 1507–8, 14 pounds was paid on 1 February to Barton for 'ane gun to the King.'[23] A few days later, on 14 February, the King shot the 'gret gunnis' in the Abbey close – three gunners were in attendance and 18 shillings was given to them.[24] Since there was not money subsequently paid for the repair of the Abbey this payment was perhaps for being skilled enough to ensure that the King didn't damage anything too important! A few months later James who was clearly interested in guns, had a culverin made for him by a priest, Sir Peter. He also began to shoot, or at least attempt to shoot, birds and deer with these guns.[25] The same year, various equipment was also bought for the guns:

> 'for tua sersouris [sieves] for gun powdir'; ramrods for the guns, 'For j ram of lattoun [brass] and tua of steil for the Kingis culverin,'[26] 'ii stane of Orkney butter,'[27] 'pellokis [shot] to the kingis culveryn'[28]

and a gunner's quadrant to allow the gunners to calculate the angle for elevating the larger guns. 'iij unce brint silvir to mak iij quadrantis for gunnis.'[29] Gunners used the quadrant to calculate the gun's angle of elevation. A cannon firing at a 45 degree angle could fire up to 10 times further than a gun fired on the level. This is surprisingly early for the use of quadrants in artillery.

In 1509, James bought guns on the Continent. In February 1510, Henry VIII's agent, Thomas Spinelly, wrote that he had made a deal with Hans Popenroyter of Mechelen for guns at a better price than those that had been sold to the Scots. Henry suggested that he might try to procure the guns meant for the Scots, however since they were brought to Scotland by George Paterson

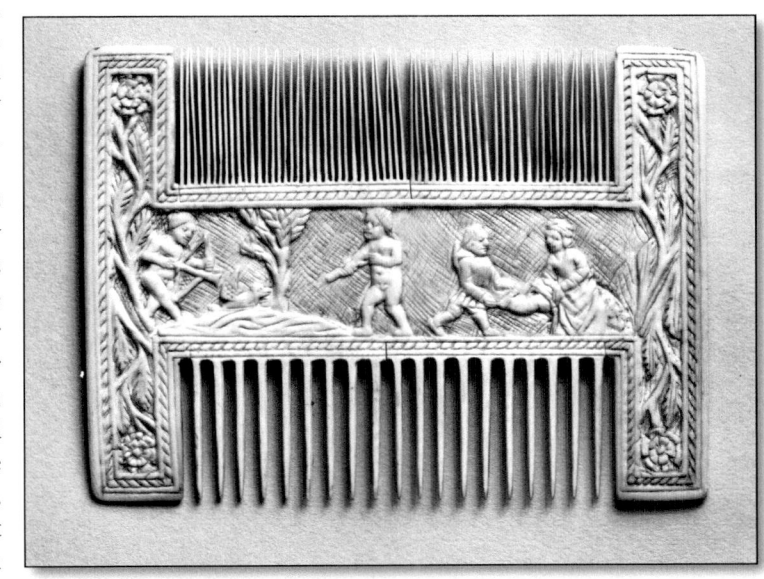

Ivory comb, French, c1500. On the left, two nude boys, one with a bow and the other with a hand cannon, shoot at a sitting duck. On the right, a youth pulls off the stocking of a seated woman. (© Walters Museum)

---

23 1508 TA IV 99 .
24 Ib 100.
25 D. H. Caldwell, 'Royal Patronage of Arms and Armour Making in Fifteenth and Sixteenth Century Scotland', D. Caldwell (ed.), *Scottish Weapons and Fortifications* (Edinburgh, John Donald, 1981), p.80. 'Sir' is a courtesy title given to priest.
26 1513 Ib IV III.
27 Used for greasing the wheels. 1513 TA IV 515.
28 1508 TA IV 102.
29 1506 TA IV 110.

65

of Leith in October 1511, this was clearly not successful.[30] In March 1511, £7 was paid to George Paterson for the shipping of 144 cannonballs (*gunestanis*).[31] These were iron cannonballs that the Scots struggled to make in any quantity themselves.

In 1508 the casting of bronze guns was restarted at Stirling and then, in 1511, the industry moved to Edinburgh. A great cannon with the unambiguous name of *Necar* [to decapitate or kill] was cast in 1511. Theoretically, this gun could have had a weight of as much as 5,400 pounds [approximately 2.449 metric tons].[32] In July 1511, a gunpowder mill, 'ane powdir myll', was imported for the King from Flanders to Dundee by Dundee burgess, James Wedderburn, at a cost of £3 12s.[33] In April 1512, six bemys [probably shining] culverings were sent to Leith by James Simpson of Flanders with William Brownhill of Campvere (the staple port of Scotland), once again these were sent with George Patterson. Shining handguns implies that these guns were metal. He also imported another 318 cannonballs (*pellokis*) weighing 6,300 pounds [2.86 metric tons].[34] In December of the year before Flodden funds were paid to John, the quarrier, for stone cannonballs (gwnstanes) for the bombards *Tabard* and the *Gun of Threave*.[35] Money was also paid to 13 workmen, who were working with Robin Borthwick, Rob Scot and Wolf at the gunpowder mill in 1513.

Pitscottie, wrote in his 16th century history that Robert Borthwick, James IV's master gun maker and based in Edinburgh Castle, had cast seven large guns that were lost to the English at Flodden.[36] The artillery train lost at that battle included seven large guns, described in contemporary accounts as five cannon and two grose culverins, four culverin pikmoyens, six culverin moyens and probably other small guns as well.[37] This included several bronze cannon some of which had been delivered from France and some of the pieces bought from Hans Popenroyter the previous year.[38] These were the shipments of iron gun shot from Campvere, two in 1511 and a third in July 1512.[39] 'The 'kingis gunnis' and… pinouris.'[40]

The siege train for Norham Castle comprised 17 pieces, and many cannon were also supplied to the fleet.[41] On 18 August, the artillery set off from Scotland. There is a long list in the Treasurer's Accounts giving the

---

30   D. H. Caldwell, 'James IV at Land and Sea', p.45.
31   1511 TA IV 288.
32   1511 TA IV 278. 'To the furnesing and casting of ane gret canoun callit the Necar cassin (cast) this day.'
33   1511 TA IV 292.
34   1512 TA IV 301.
35   1512 TA IV 460.
36   Pitscottie, *History* 1, pp.259–60.
37   D. H. Caldwell, 'James IV at Land and Sea', p.60. 1513 TA, IV 518.
38   D. H. Caldwell, 'Royal Patronage of Arms and Armour', p.77.
39   1511/12 TA IV, 301–3 and 305.
40   1512 TA IV 302.
41   1513 T A, IV, 451–507, 515–518, 527.

number of drivers needed, the workmen required and their tools. 'The first canone drawin with the captane of the castellis oxin…with this canone xx werkmen with x schulis, v pikis, and v spaidis.'[42] Additionally a crane for mounting and dismounting the guns followed, pulled by eight oxen and a horse with three drivers.[43] There was also a diversionary tactic of attempting to send some artillery pieces to Ireland. Five cannon and culverin moyen and two carts with eight barrels of powder, two carts with gunstones, one with pikes, shovels and mattocks and a crane along with the trestles on which the cannon was to be mounted were sent to Glasgow but unfortunately for the King returned too late to be of any use at Flodden.[44] On 19 August, two great culverins and four culverins, 'twa gros culveringis and four culvering pikmoyance', left the Castle to leave Edinburgh through the Saint Mary's Wynd [the nethir port of Sanct Mary Wynd].[45] St Mary's Wynd no longer exists since it was demolished in 1860 in the slum clearance, but much of the army and artillery for Flodden left from there.

The largest artillery pieces that James had at his disposal were cannons and double cannons, these were essentially siege weapons designed for bringing down town walls. Smaller than these, but still formidable, were the culverins, which, although of a smaller bore, were relatively longer in length, giving them greater range than the larger guns. Smaller in size than all of these guns were the various falcons and 'hagbuts of crok', the latter had hooks on the underside of their barrels, instead of trunnions, for mounting them.[46]

James' request to King Louis XII of France for guns and equipment had resulted in a ship arriving in Scotland on 30 November 1512 carrying the French ambassador, Charles de Tocque, Seigneur de la Mothe, and in de la Mothe's party was one of the Louis XII's gunners, Jehan Piefort, who may have taken part in the Flodden campaign. There was also a large amount of guns, shot and powder. Eight hundred iron cannon balls and 15,000 pounds (6.8 metric tonnes) of gunpowder as well as what English sources described as ten large brass guns, eight of which are supposed to have fired shot the size of a swan's egg.[47] There were also 28 horses with creels loaded with gunstones, 'xxviij hors with creilis…to cary gun stanis.'[48] 15 hired carts with powder, shot and other equipment, and two closed carts. Robert Bothwick had 26 men under him carrying his ramrods, 'To bere his chargeouris'[49]

The range of the guns that the Scots had was impressive as was the technology available to them – the Scots development of artillery was at

---

42   1513 TA IV, 519.
43   1513 TA IV, 515.
44   Ibid 520.
45   1513 *TA* IV 516, 17.
46   D. H. Caldwell, 'James IV at Land and Sea', p.44.
47   Swans lay huge eggs. They are about 12cm x 7cm in size and have a weight of around 350g,
48   1513 TA IV 517.
49   1513 TA IV 519.

THE MEN OF WARRE

the forefront of the European mainstream. Despite the three heaviest cannons having been left somewhere along the way, most likely at Norham, although Etal is also possible, Thomas Howard writes about the grace and high quality finish of the Scots guns.[50] The double cannon had a maximum range of 1,500 yards (1371.6metres); and the cannon 1,700 yards (1554.48 metres).

Although the heavier pieces could potentially overheat if fired too often and this restricted their rate of fire, the lighter pieces could be fired as often as they could be loaded. The tragedy for the Scots at Flodden was that despite the excellent hardware they had no experienced gunners to operate their artillery, their most experienced men were with the fleet. However, by Flodden the Scots had been casting excellent bronze guns for some time. They had also been experimenting successfully with culverin powder – gunpowder mixed with whisky. 'Gevin for x li. of colvering powder to the Kingis grace.'[51]

The army at Flodden had two silk banners – of St Andrew and of St Margaret, 'four ellis of blew taffeteis to mak Sanct Androwis and Sanct Margrettis baneris.' While the King's standard was made of four ells of red silk, with his Arms embroidered and not painted on it, 'To browdin [embroider] the kingis armes apoun the said standartis.'[52] These flags all had silk fringes. 'iiij unce of sewing silk to be frenzeis to the baneris and standartis'[53] 'For … silk to be fren3eis [fringe] to the baneris and standartis.'[54] There is also mention of the Saltire 'flag' for the first time, 'xxiiij ellis lynnyng [Linen] to lit blew for the heid of the standert to pant Sanct Androis cors. Saint Andrew Cross painted on the standard.'[55] A banner meant a rectangular flag. It seems likely that the King's red standard was the red lion rampant on a gold field.

The flag of 3rd Earl Marischal of Scotland was carried onto the field by his standard bearer, 'Black' John Skirving, of Plewlandhill, East Lothian. It had three stag heads and the motto, *Veritas Vincit* (Truth will conquer). He managed to retain it and keep it hidden during his time in captivity after Flodden and eventually he, and the standard, returned to Scotland. It is now on display in the Faculty of Advocates in Edinburgh.

The best known of the guild banners that could have been on the field at Flodden is the 'Blue Blanket' of the Incorporated Trades of Edinburgh. The legend says the banner was presented to the craftsmen of Edinburgh in 1482 by King James III, after they had rescued him from Edinburgh Castle, where he had been imprisoned, however there is no verified document of the period that records this supposed event. The banner was blue, hence the

---

50   P. Reese, *Flodden: A Scottish Tragedy*, (Edinburgh, Birlinn, 2013), quoted on p.75.
51   1536 TA VI 436.
52   1512 TA IV 369.
53   1513 TA IV 521.
54   1513 TA IV 521.
55   1513 TA IV 477.

nickname, with a saltire, crown, thistle and an extremely long motto, *Fear God and honour ye King with a lyffe and a prosperous reign and we shall ever pray to be faithful for ye defence of his sacred Royal Majesty until death.*[56]

In 1513, two shillings were given to John Hartside, a pavilion man, who had been working on the pavilions with four servants, (taking 1s 4d daily) for three weeks preparing for the campaign.[57] Additionally, two shoemakers were paid eight shillings each to dress skins for the King's pavilion. Tents were also made for the heralds and for Robert Borthwick, the Master Gunner. Forty men, whose duty was to erect these tents, travelled with the army.[58]

The Captain of Edinburgh Castle presented a report to the Queen Dowager in 1514, 'the castel quhil is ane of the principale strenthis of the realme is now desolat of artalery and utherthing is necessar for defens.'[59] After the defeat at Flodden, provision was made promptly to unload the artillery from the Scottish ships at Dumbarton, there were at least 14 pieces of artillery, large and small, including the two great cannon, and have them moved to Edinburgh. John Stewart, Regent Albany, himself brought several guns and there was a great deal of activity at Holyrood Palace that summer with craftsmen working on close carts, gun stocks and palyeons [tents]. 'xxxj wrichtis, certane sawaris, masounis, smythtis and uthir workmen wirk and on my lord governournis close cartis, gunnys, and gun stokkis.' Pitscottie's claim that the six cannon, six great field pieces and other small artillery, culverins, hagbuts and crossbows were brought with the Duke of Albany is quite probably correct.[60]

In 1515, gun founding restarted at Edinburgh Castle, 'To Robin of Borthwick, master founder gunnar, to furnisss tokkis, irne, charcoal and uthir necessaris for the founding of certane gunnys.'[61] In May 1526, a payment of 20 pounds was made to Borthwick as part-payment for four small artillery pieces (iiij smal pecis of artalzere) that were being made in the castle.[62] There are also payments for the carriages, wheels and fittings. Clearly working and testing continued, as a few years later, a payment of 40 shillings was recorded as made to a woman whose husband had been killed by a gunshot from the Castle.[63]

---

56 The 'Blue Blanket Banner' is in the Museum of Incorporated Trades, Edinburgh. However, the first definitive mention of it is in 1543 and that seems to assume prior knowledge so there's a reasonable possibility that it, or a banner very like it, was indeed at Flodden.
57 1513 TA IV 503.
58 Hodge, *Edinburgh Castle Research*, p.196.
59 Ibid p.200.
60 1515 TA, V,14–15, 17 and 38; Pitscottie, Historie, vol. I, p.288, Caldwell, D H 'James IV at Land and Sea, p66
61 1515 TA V 18–19.
62 1526 TA V 266.
63 1532 TA VI 4.

In 1523, Regent Albany returned from France to carry out an ultimately unsuccessful campaign against England. In a letter to Surrey dated 29 September, Margaret Tudor, who should have had access to reliable intelligence, wrote that he (the Regent Albany) has twenty-eight cannon, and four double cannons:

> … greater than ony that vass browht to Noram at the feld. Allsua he hath gret pavasys [great pavises] gangan a pon vhylyz vyth the artylery to schwt [to pass]and to brek the hostys syndre; and of thys he hath mony, and every een of them hath tway scharpe befoor them that nen may tawsche them. [every one of them hath two sharp swords before them that none may touch them]'
>
> They have also much smaller artillery with ample ammunition, and twelve ships with victual and wine. They have sent four to the West Borders with four great cannons. There have arrived 4,000 foot, 100 men of arms, and 80 'bardyd [armoured] hors.[64]

On the 7 October another report came from:

> Sir Wm. Bulmer, has spoken with the prioress of Eklyn [Eccles], who told him that the Duke brought with him to Dunbarton 87 ships, 100 barded horses, 500 light horses, 4,000 foot, 500 men of arms, and 1,000 hagbusshis, and had 900 serpentines and fawcons, 16 great guns, called cannons, and gunpowder to the value of 10,000 crowns' weight, and came to Glasgow with a privy company, and thence to Stirling.

This was obviously exaggerated. Albany's carts appear to have been closed, and able to take eight men, The mention of pavises (shields) and the steel and brass further reinforces this idea, while Queen Margaret's description of the swords in front of the cart, gives the impression that the carts were pushed from behind by their armoured horses, rather being than pulled.[65] These carts appear to have been intended almost like tanks, designed to push through infantry and break their ranks.

In 1528, a siege train of four thirty-six pound guns (16.39 kilograms) and a battard (a form of culverin) were able to leave Edinburgh Castle for the magnificent Tantallon Castle in East Lothian. The castle eventually surrendered to King.

---

64   D. H. Caldwell, 'James IV at Land and Sea', p.67. N. Murphy, 'The Duke of Albany's Invasion of England in 1523 and Military Mobilisation in Sixteenth-Century Scotland', *The Scottish Historical Review 2020* 99:1 (Edinburgh, 2020), pp. 1–25.

65   D. H. Caldwell, 'James IV at Land and Sea', p.68.

Horse barding. Much lighter, faster and cheaper to produce than metal defences, armour made from shaped and hardened leather was used throughout Europe for war. In 1547, for example, the Master of the Armoury at the Tower of London bought forty-six "leather barbes" (bards) for an imminent campaign in Scotland so it is possible that some of Albany's barded horses were wearing leather armour. (© Metropolitian Museum of Art)

6

The Borders – 'Na, we's all Elliots and Armstrongs' [1]

> bold and gallant enough, but are not so well armed as the French, for they have very little well made, clean and polished armour, but use jackets of mail in exercising daily with the French, and have the custom of using little ambling nags and small horses; their lances are small and narrow, and they have scarce any large horses, and few are brought to them, except from France.[2]

Until at least the end of the 16th century, the Borders were a place apart. The men there very often held their loyalty to their families and the place, rather than to their country. This led to various accusations more than once. In 1525 for example, it was noted that the 'Armystrangs of Liddersdaill and the thieves of Ewysdaill consort with the Tynedale rebels.'[3]

The preparations before the invasion of 1482 by Richard, Duke of Gloucester were careful. Parliament, ordered that wappenschaws should be increased in frequency to every 15 days and the coastline was to be split into six mile (9.7 kilometre) stretches, each under a captain, 'to gadir the cuntre and to awayte thareuppoune quhen thare is na grete hoisting is be hadd.'[4]

---

1 A 16th century visitor, 'Are there no Christians in Liddesdale?' To which he was answered 'Na, we's all Elliots and Armstrongs.' This may in fact have been a coded reference to the fact that Reformation was quite slow to penetrate the Borders, and well after 1560, there remained many Catholics.
2 D. H. Caldwell, 'Some Notes on Scottish shafted weapons,' p.255.
3 Henry VIII: May 1525, 11–20', in *Letters and Papers, Foreign and Domestic, Henry VIII, Volume 4,* pp.583–595. [Accessed 25 October 2022].
4 RPS, record 1482/3/44. J. W. Armstrong, 'Local Society and the Defence of the English Frontier in Fifteenth Century Scotland', p.132.

THE BORDERS – 'NA, WE'S ALL ELLIOTS AND ARMSTRONGS'

However, a land attack was expected. While the King undertook to pay for a garrison of five hundred soldiers to defend Berwick for three months from the beginning of June, the estates agreed to pay for a further six hundred 'wageouris' to garrison other castles and towers for three months from the first day of May. Half of the men were spearmen and half archers. No horsemen were provided since apparently there were already plenty of those in the Borders. Landed men serving in the feudal levy were expected to be well horsed, according to their means. Non-elite men in the Borders in particular, commonly rode in the retinues of local lairds, riding unarmoured 'hobbies'. It seems that the additional garrisons of 1482, providing extra archers and spearmen to guard certain towers, would have concurrently allowed other Borderers to serve on horseback in private retinues.[5] This was the pattern that continued for the next hundred years. Scottish mounted troops were generally recruited from Borders, and these troops were normally used for raiding and reconnaissance. Their expertise was also highly prized by the French.[6] The issue being the times when the men in Borders raided each other, or deep into England or sometimes when the fancy or necessity took them into Scotland.

Northern horsemen were looked for by the English for service in Ireland, as indeed were 'Northumberland speres, light fote men, apte to take payn and labours, as the marchers of Scotland and the men of warr of this contre.'[7]

Patten's description of the Borderers at Pinkie is unflattering but gives the idea that he thinks that they may have had more loyalty to each other than to the countries that they were ostensibly fighting for. He described them as, 'our Northern prickers, the Borderers'. Prickers as they were probably fighting with a lance and definitely on horseback. The Borderers used fairly small, hardy horses. They were particularly important to the Scots as cavalry since Patten went on to say that before the battle 'they were hooping…whistling, and most with crying, a Berwick! a Berwick! a FENWICK! a FENWICK! A BULMER! a BULMER!' Patten described that they wore 'hand Kerchers rolled about their arms, and letters broidered upon their caps.' He makes it clear that he felt that they were wearing them to identify themselves to other Borderers so they wouldn't kill each other accidentally, 'in conflict, either each to spare the other, or gently each to take the other.'[8] He also suggests that their crosses, showing that they were English could just blow off, 'and that were found, right often, talking with the Scottish prickers within less than their gads [spears] length asunder.'

---

5   RPS, record 1482/3/44. J. W. Armstrong, 'Local Society and the Defence of the English Frontier in Fifteenth Century Scotland', p.133.

6   G. Phillips, 'Scotland in the Age of Military Revolution, 1488–1560', J. A. Crang, E. M. Spiers, & M. J. Strickland (Eds) *A Military History of Scotland*, (Edinburgh, Edinburgh University Press, 2014) pp.182–207, at p.187.

7   State .Papers Hen. VIII, ii, 146

8   W. Patten, 'The Expedition into Scotland, p.134.

This demonstrated the strong family loyalty that many in Borders had to each other regardless of the country they were supposed to be loyal to.

In 1578, men in the Borders were described in the Privy Council Register as, 'bodin with Jakkis, steilbonettis, pistolettis, speris, lang hagbuts and Jedburgh staffs.'[9] An inventory of goods stolen from a servant of Sir John Forster in 1590 gives his possessions as 'two doublets, a cloak, a jerkin…a five pairs of linen sheets, two coverlets, two linen shirts.'[10] The Borderers, as can be seen from the inventory, didn't dress any differently from any other Lowlander. A steel bonnet, or towards the end of the century a morion – if the man was wealthier this might have been gilded or covered in fabric, 'to Johnie Moubray, burgess of Edinburght, for ane giltin murione.'[11]

Doublet and breeches with cloth hose or 'schankis', 'Ane pair of blew brekis with ane pair of blew schankis.'[12] Blue being a particularly favourite colour for poorer men since it was cheap and was allowed under the sumptuary laws that remained in force in Scotland. Land owning men or men who felt they had some status would wear darker colours, generally black. Forster's servant also has linen shirts or sarks and the quality and amount of linen would vary depending on social class. The majority of men would be wearing flat knitted hats which could be blue but black, red and brown were also seen. A higher status man might wear a 'how-bonet', woollen or velvet hat with a stiff brim and a high crown. A black how bonet appears in the Peebles Court records in 1560. In the latter part of the 16th century, these men would almost certainly be wearing ruffs. Higher status individuals would have had trimming on their doublets and hose. They frequently wore a 'jack of plates' over their doublet when riding – probably similar to the extant example in the Royal Armouries.[13]

The 'jack of plates' had small, overlapping square plates (generally with cropped corners), each with a central hole through which it was stitched to an inner and an outer padding. From the outside, all that could be seen of the hidden metal plates was the cross-stitching. The 'jack of plates' was not medieval, it was seen only from the 16th century and most commonly in England and Scotland.[14] Legislation of 1540 decreed that lower status men should have one 'haif jak of plait, halbrek or brigitanis, gorget or pisane.'[15] Relatively few pairs of riding boots are extant from the 16th century and those that do exist are knee or thigh high. Spurs were worn when riding,

---

9   M. Kelvin, *The Scottish Pistol*.
10 George MacDonald Fraser, *The Steel Bonnets: The Story of the Angle Scottish Border Reivers* (London, Pan Books, 1974), p.54.
11 C. Whitelaw, *Scottish Arms Makers*, p.77.
12 "Shank *n*.". *Dictionary of the Scots Language*. 2004. Scottish Language Dictionaries Ltd. Accessed 2 Nov 2021.
13 https://collections.royalarmouries.org/object/rac-object–16361.html.
14 R. Moffat, 'Jack', *Encyclopaedia of Medieval Dress and Textiles*, Edited by: G. Owen-Crocker, E. Coatsworth, M. Hayward (Eds). Consulted online, 07 May 2022.
15 1540 RPS II 362/2.

THE BORDERS – 'NA, WE'S ALL ELLIOTS AND ARMSTRONGS'

there were 'arming' spurs worn with harness, and gilt or red (gold) spurs which were the mark or a knight or nobility.

Small crossbows, known as latchets, had been developed for use by horse by the 16th century. The Border horsemen used these relatively light crossbows, which could be loaded with one hand while holding the reins with the other, and these were probably more reliable than the clumsy pistols of the period.[16] Larger crossbows were often owned by towns in the Borders and the Lothians, and armourers, and later gunmakers, were frequently called upon to maintain them. There was also the pellok bow, which shot lead pellets, or stones, 'Deliverit to Johne Tennand thre pellok bowis.' This was probably used more for hunting but may well have been employed in the kind of raiding and skirmishing that the Borderers frequently took part in.

In 1540, legislation stated that that, in order to avoid the destruction of crops, the army of the Kingdom of Scotland was to be horseless except for the great barons; although it does not say so in the legislation, the Borderers were not included in this. The King clearly expected the majority of his army to be on foot carrying long spears or pikes, supported by the Borderers' cavalry. In a national emergency for Scotland, such as Pinkie, the penchant of the Borderers for raiding and feuding allowed the quick raising of a highly-skilled light cavalry force. This fortunate circumstance was described in a Minute in the papers of the Privy Council in October 1545 when three commissioners were given the responsibility of raising 1,000 horsemen to 'pass and remain upon the Borders for the space of three months for defence of the realm against our old enemy of England.' It was noted that they would be paid from an allotted sum of £18,000 Scots.[17]

Borderers carried spears or lances on horseback, a sword (probably a winger, an early basket hilt or a variation on the Lowland claymore). By the later 16th century, anyone who could afford it would also almost certainly also have a firearm. In 1600, in Peebles James Dikkson killed James Glaidstanes of Cokilaw with the 'schott of ane pistollet and straikis of swordis and lanceis'.

They would also have carried a dagger, generally a bollock type with a wooden handle, the word dudgeon is often used to describe the stock or haft, 'To Alexander Wicht, cultellar, for … four duggeoun-stokkis.'[18] The type of wood and amount of decoration was dependent on status so non-elite men carried daggers with handles made from

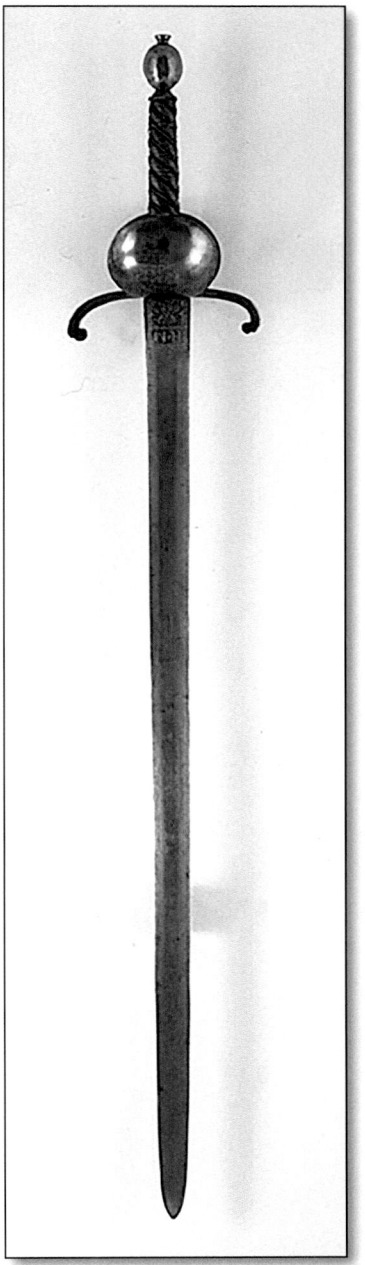

A clamshell claymore c1600, engraved with the initials and coat of arms of Murray of Tullibardine. Taken to Sweden in the 17th century. (© Swedish Royal Armouries)

---

16 M. Loades, *The Crossbow*, (Oxford, Osprey Publishing, 2018), p.35. Leo Todeschini of 'Tod's Stuff' has made a replica of this crossbow and it can be viewed on his website.

17 J. Miller, *The Scottish Mercenary as Migrant Labour in Europe 1550–1660, Fighting for a Living : A Comparative Study of Military Labour 1500–2000*, E. Zürcher (ed.), (Amsterdam, Amsterdam University Press, 2014), p 179.

18 1541 TA VIII 54

native woods and those of higher status had imported wood and inlays of silver, frequently with a double-edged diamond shaped blade which might have an inscription on it. These blades, like the majority of sword blades were often imported.

Most people did not make their own clothes, the exception generally being body linens, which the women of the household were normally expected to sew. However, many of the clothes working class men wore in the Borders as elsewhere in Scotland would not necessarily have been new to them, although servants were often given clothes or cloth as part of their pay, and individuals might also inherit clothes from a dead master or mistress. Children frequently had clothes remade from their parents' or older siblings' clothing, this happened across the social spectrum and there were also second hand markets in many of the big towns throughout Scotland. Chepmen would walk through the Borders and elsewhere carrying linen, buttons, thread and ribbons (although not tobacco until the end of the 16th century). 'Diuers vnfremen [not a burgess or a guildman of the town], chepmen, cowparis, [cooper] and vtheris dailie occupies.'[19]

Bishop Leslie described the Borderers travelling through:

> their territory in bands, through pathless places and with many twists. During the day they refresh their horses and their own strength in pre-determined hiding places… Having seized the booty, they similarly return by night to their own land by circuitous by-ways. … they possess such skill that very rarely do they allow their booty to be snatched from them, except that sometimes they are taken by their adversaries if they are led by scent-following dogs [in the vernacular Sleuth-hounds or Bloodhounds].[20]

In 1586, the Privy Council decided that armed men were required to police the Borders. They would be paid £20 a month for a horseman, £6 for a foot soldier and nearly £70 and £50 for their captains respectively.[21]

---

19 "Chepman n.". *Dictionary of the Scots Language*. 2004. Scottish Language Dictionaries Ltd. (Accessed 23 Nov 2022).
20 This is from Bishop Leslie's 16th century *Historie of Scotland* and is quoted in the *Blaeu Atlas of Scotland*, 1654 in the description of Nithsdale. By 1654, of course the Borders had been pacified.
21 J. Miller, *The Scottish Mercenary*, p.191.

7

Fire and sword

> Put all to fire and sword, burn Edinburgh, so razed and defaced when you have sacked and gotten what ye can of it, as there may remain forever a perpetual memory of the vengeance of God lightened upon [them] for their falsehood and disloyalty[1]

The Act of Parliament of 1535 and of five years later in 1540, enjoined the gentry to furnish themselves with a hagbut of crok or an arquebus, and bullets, 'Euery landit man … sall haue ane hagbute of found callit hagbute of crochert with thar cawmys, bullettis and pellokis off leid or irne'.[2] There is little evidence that these small pieces were ever taken to wappenshaws, raids or elsewhere with the Royal army although quite considerable numbers were being brought into Scotland. In 1541, John Drummond received 130 lightweight handguns (half haggis), 64 hand-culverins (culveringis), 103 powder horns (hornis), 220 slow match (luntis) and two barrels of culverin powder.[3] As can be seen, the smaller guns are mostly variations of hagbuts, which were sometimes called a harquebus. 'Bullettis, hagbuttis and uthir small geir.'[4]

Later in 1541, John Drummond, the Master Gunner at Edinburgh Castle took receipt of another 413 small handguns (half haggis), 412 sets of bullet moulds (calmes), 62 powder horns, 413 powder flasks (flassis) and 407 slow-matches (luntis), plus eight muskets (culveringis) with their bullet moulds, and three barrels of powder.[5] In this delivery, Drummond received much of paraphernalia that would actually allow him to use his guns: bullet

---

1   L. Mickel, L "Our Hielandmen,' Scots in Court Entertainment at Home and Abroad 1307 – 1618', Journal for the Society of Renaissance Studies, volume 33, issue 2 (Wiley, 2019), pp. 185–203. Henry VIII's order is quoted on p.186.
2   RPS 1535 II 345/2, 1540 Ib 371/2
3   1541 TA VII. 498.
4   1540 TA VII 354.
5   1541 TA VIII 120.

moulds to cast lead bullets easily, powder horns (many of these were actual horns with stoppers), powder flasks were often made of leather or wood in a wedge shape with an iron frame, iron spout and rings for suspension from twine or thin rope. The next year, a payment of £6 was made to Richard Seton for 400 chargers for the small handguns, these are either ramrods or perhaps small wooden powder flasks that some men were beginning to wear in bandoliers.[6]

Only a relatively small number of big guns seem to have been available for sieges in the 1540s after the King's death, when Scotland was once more at war with England. A small siege train led by a single cannon left Edinburgh to besiege Glasgow in 1543, and again to attack Coldingham in the Borders. Some of the lack of guns was because some had been moved elsewhere to contain possible trouble.

Larger artillery was the concern of the King. There is a small falcon with James V's initials in the collection of the Glasgow Museums, which is one of the few to survive from this period. In the early 1550s, not long after Pinkie, the gun foundry at Edinburgh Castle was producing small bronze guns, a few of which do still survive, 'grete hagbuttis of found' or 'doubil hagbuttis of fund.'[7]

An inventory of Edinburgh Castle in March 1566/7 gives some idea of its defence, and probably was little different a few years later during the siege. There were 26 artillery pieces in the castle. On the forewall there were four new French cannons mounted on carriages, as were the two grose culverins. On top of David's Tower there was a moyen also mounted on a carriage. At the back of the munition house were two bastards, and below the hill, two further cannons. At either end of the chapel were four pieces; two cannons and two moyens, or at the western end of the rock, there was a saker and a falcon. Between the butts, there was a double cannon, a culverin, a saker, two moyens and a double falcon, and lastly, at the gunhouse gable there was a grose culverin and a moyen.[8]

The Scottish Crown may have had at its disposal in the later part of the 16th century somewhere in the region of 80 large cast bronze or iron guns, some sizeable wrought iron pieces and other smaller pieces.[9] Two of the best known guns of the period, the two big siege guns with Albany's coat of Arms, were probably known at the time as *Thrawn Mouth* and *Little Thrawn Mouth*. The two guns had been the main Scottish guns at the siege of Tantallon in 1528, and were deployed again at St Andrews Castle in 1547 and against the English fort at Haddington in 1548.[10]

---

6   1542 TA VIII 129. He also had another gunmaker, John Biykkerton working on the 'auld culveringis' replacing the ramrods ibid 128

7   1552/3 TA X 110, 115.

8   T. Thomson (ed.), *Wardrobe Inventories. A Collection of Inventories and other Records of the Royal Wardrobe and Jewel House* (Edinburgh, 1815), pp.165–77.

9   D. Caldwell, 'The Defence of the Scottish Border,' p.77.

10   A. Hodge, *Edinburgh Castle: The Medieval Documents*, p.515. Thrawn means twisted.

Many pikes were imported into Scotland in the years before Pinkie and Solway Moss. Four hundred and forty-eight pikes of Spanish ash and one hundred and seven pikes of white ash each with their spearheads (iiiicxlviij pikkis of Spanzeesche and icvij pikkis, quhite esche hedit), a further forty-two pike shafts of white ash and twelve pike shafts of beech (xlij pikkis quite esche, and xij pikkis of beche, unhedit).[11] In addition to these pikes, there were 3,500 pikes and 466 halberds, to repair which a thousand nails were bought.[12] 'ane thows and takkettis, bocht be him to mend the faitis of iijv pikkis and xxiiijvj halbertis.'

In 1543, after the defeat of Solway Moss and the death of James V, a French observer noted that not only were the nobility in arms:

> but churchmen, friars and country people only travel through the countryside in large companies all armed with pikes, swords and bucklers and a half pike in their hands, which in this country is called a lance.[13]

Wappenshaws still had to be held regularly and were held still more frequently as war became more likely. Both football and golf were banned and men were, instead, supposed to practice archery, but there is some evidence from court books that men were fined for non-attendance at the wappenshaws implying that not everyone was keen to attend.

In the years after Solway Moss and Pinkie the wearing of handguns by men who were not soldiers became fashionable. Many ordinary men had seen violence, 'Thomas Schort was crewilly slane with our auld innemies of Ingland at their invasion and buryng of this burgh…he was slane with a goune fechand at the Nedder Port in defence'.[14] There were frequent bans, however 'the town of Edinburgh was always is exemptit.'[15] This is perhaps a lesson in perception as it appears that it is the men in the Lowlands, and in particular Edinburgh, who were going about armed with handguns and not the apparently violent Highlanders. This is further reinforced, as in the 1550s the town of Edinburgh banned men from carrying 'lang walpynnis [weapons] thairin, sic as hand ex, jedburgh staif, halbart, jawalyng [halberds, javelins] and siclik lang walpynnis with knaipskawis and jakkis, [and using them with knapsculls and jacks]' which does rather imply all

---

11 1541 T A. VII. 498.
12 1541/2 TA VII xxi.
13 D. H. Caldwell. 'Some Notes on Scottish Shafted Weapons', p.255.
14 Whitelaw, Scottish Arms Makers p79. The Nedder Port is the Netherbow Port on the Royal Mile of Edinburgh.
15 T. Thomson (ed.), *Diurnal of the remarkable occurents that have passed within the country of Scotland since the death of James the Fourth till the year MDLXXV* (1575), (Edinburgh, Bannatyre Club, 1833) p.163. D. H. Caldwell, 'Royal Patronage of Arms and Armour', p.92, note.

out fighting on the streets.[16] Whitelaw lists a large number of dag or gun makers in Edinburgh and Dundee, and later in the 16th century, Glasgow and St Andrews.[17] 'The gunmakeris [are to make] hagbuttis and daggis' in Dundee.[18] Pistols were in Scotland by 1549 when two Dutchmen wounded a Scotsman in Stirling.[19] By the 1570s, an English spy stated that the Regent has bought:

> six fair muskets [from] Flanders to serve for patterns … for which purpose his artificers are skilful and as for dagges, [otherwise called] 'snaphaunces' [and that they have]   furnished the most part of the gentlemen and horsemen of the realm.'[20]

In 1594, the essay to complete apprenticeship for the Edinburgh Hammermen was 'a hackbut and a dag'.[21]

In 1583, Robert Lyal was admitted as a guardmaker for swords and made a pair of clam shaped guards for a sword, generally seen on a Lowland claymore. He also made skellit gairds [bell shaped], and ane pair ribbit [ribbon] guards, both often seen on the rapier type swords that were beginning to emerge at this time.[22] The Edinburgh lorimers agreed fixed prices for 'Londoun gairdis, slycht [light English] Inglis gairdis with others' in 1593.[23] Alexander Grub, an armourer in Edinburgh who died in 1585, had 'small ribbit' guards. 'Lundoun' guards, braid stittit (probably actually slittit) guards, Inglis guards, slyt ribbit guards, quheild [wheel] guards, losane [diamond].[24] These guards were fitted onto blades, which had for the most part been imported from Germany, by sword slippers to make the finished sword.

---

16   J. D. Marwick (ed.), *Records of the Burgh of Edinburgh, 1528–1557*, (Edinburgh, Scottish Burgh Records Society, 1871), *British History Online*, http://www.british-history.ac.uk/edinburgh-burgh-records/1528–57/pp175–186   [accessed 25 October 2021.

17   M. Kelvin, *The Scottish Pistol*, (London, Cyrus Arts, 1996), p.68. The first gun maker in St Andrews is recorded in 1585.

18   "Gun *n.*". *Dictionary of the Scots Language*. 2004. Scottish Language Dictionaries Ltd. Accessed 25 Oct 2022 <http://www.dsl.ac.uk/entry/dost/gun

19   D. H. Caldwell, *Royal Patronage of Arms and Armour*, p.90.

20   J. Bain, W. K. Boyd, H. W. Meikle, A. I. Cameron, M. S. Guiseppi, and J. D. Mackie (eds), *Calendar of the State Papers relating to Scotland and Mary Queen of Scots, 1547–1603*, (Glasgow H.M. General Register House) Volume IX.

21   M. Kelvin *The Scottish Pistol*, p.66. In 1586 a founder, David Williamson had produced 'ane hagbuit mesour' for his ticket for burgesship which implies standardisation

22   "Lorimar *n.*". *Dictionary of the Scots Language*. 2004. Scottish Language Dictionaries Ltd. Accessed 25 Oct 2021 <http://www.dsl.ac.uk/entry/dost/lorimar

23   C. A. Whitelaw, S. Baxter (eds), *Scottish Arms Makers…* p.19.

24   C. A. Whitelaw, S. Baxter (eds), *Scottish Arms Makers…* p.19.

The Master Gunner in 1541 had a cloak of French black, hose and a doublet of black velvet.[25] The Scots were very well supplied at Pinkie with artillery, although somewhat lacking in experienced gunners despite their smart livery. Michael Gardiner, another gunner who moved from Edinburgh Castle Garrison to Stirling in the 1560s, gives a glimpse of their equipment. He had a suit of armour (in reality this was more likely to be a back and breastplate rather than a whole suit) a skullcap, a hat to wear over the skullcap, spurs a sword belt and a halberd. This implied he must sometimes have ridden a horse and have had a sword.[26] Gloves were required for firing a gun. It was quite common to order multiple pairs of gloves – in one case, the Regent bought twenty-four pairs. The Treasurer's Accounts occasionally include details about the materials of the gloves. 'Fyftene pair of doubill dog ledder … gluifis'.[27] Gloves were worn for hunting, riding and shooting.

The King's household and other officers wore red and yellow livery although those above a certain status commonly received money rather than actual clothes so it is less likely they would have been wearing livery colours, although they may have had a red bonnet or possibly for war red and yellow livery coats. A knee length gown continued to be the outer layer for elite men. Gowns of silk usually velvet, damask, or satin and often lined with fur, were also worn by elite men. Gowns like these were of course restricted by the sumptuary laws to those with money and status. Most men wore coats over doublets that were laced to their hose. Some still wore wyliecoats that laced to their hose or breiks although they seem to be less prevalent than earlier in the century. Fashionable men often wore short cloth breeches or breiks, but older and/or less fashionable men continued to wear long hose cut on the bias, although these came right up to the waist rather than sitting on the hips as the earlier hose had. By the Marian wars, men were wearing short breeches and the wealthier men wore starched linen ruffs at the neck and the wrist. By the end of the century these were very large. Clean, white linen was a key mark of status.

For example in Aberdeen in 1540, Alexander Anderson had. 'a hogtone of demyostage begareit with veluet [a sleeveless jerkin of linsey-wolsey decorated with velvet], a dowblat of black satin, ane blak pair of hois stekin out with tupheit, [ornamented with tufted stitches – this could actually be stamping] ane new sark losin blak werk [decorated with black work in a diamond or square pattern.' This would only have been done on fine linen, often the embroidered bands were removable] …as well as 'a ryding coit, a ryding hat with hostrage fedders, a jak.' Given that he could afford 'hostrage fedders' it is not unreasonable to think that Anderson could also afford a

---

25 1541 TA VIII 24.
26 A. Hodge, *Edinburgh Castle: The Medieval Documents*, p.515. He also received £10 for his work in preparing the fireworks for the baptism of James VI 1566 TA XII 404
27 Gluve *n.*". *Dictionary of the Scots Language*. 2004. Scottish Language Dictionaries Ltd. Accessed 29 Nov 2021

horse, boots and some weapons. For a man like this clean linen would be important and it is unlikely that he would have ridden to the muster point without several changes of shirt, and a servant to maintain his clothes. Even the poor generally had two changes of clothes, and that legislation allowed for holy day clothes. The King had hundreds of changes of clothes and Regent Arran when he took over had many of the King's clothes altered to fit him.[28] All of this gives a good picture of the sort of clothing that a man leading one of the town contingents may have worn at Pinkie.

In 1535, John Vane, Anderson's contemporary had, 'ane gray horse witht sadill, buittis and spurris, ane sourd, ane gluif of plait, ane knapiscall, ane Dens axe.' Riding boots were expensive, as of course, was a horse. This man probably had more armour than was listed if he also owned a sword and a Dane axe. His attire means he was dressed very much like Borderers who fought on the Scots side. Many but not all the blades of the swords were imported, James Hunter from Edinburgh left Eisterling (from the Baltic or Hanseatic towns), Valentine blades (Valencia in Spain or Walloon from what is now Belgium) and Frenche blades.

Arran's trumpeter at the siege of St Andrews Castle wore a parti-coloured livery coat of scarlet and white, the livery colours of the Hamilton family, and a satin doublet,[29] but clearly, this is not what most men wore. Livery coats, such as the one worn by this trumpeter, were often parti-coloured.

By the time of Pinkie, the majority of coats opened along the centre front and had a high neckline in contrast with the earlier styles seen at Flodden, which were however still at times seen in the country and on older men – these older style coats had a low square neckline and sometimes closed at the side. Where a colour was specified in the Accounts, other than for livery coats, coats were commonly black, although less frequently violet or tawny. Of course, these records really hold information in the main about the elite, or about men of the middling sort, poorer men would still have worn clothing of undyed or lighter colours, possibly with a plaid over the top of their doublet and coat to protect against the weather.

Black was the most fashionable colour replacing scarlet and it was increasingly worn in the latter part of the 16th century as a statement of Protestant faith. However given the amount of fabrics that the sumptuary acts of 1581 felt it necessary to forbid, but that nobility, knights and landed gentlemen with an annual income of 2,000 marks, members of the King's household as well as all kinds of officials, were exempt, there must still have been a considerable market for imported silks and woollen fabrics.

The English commander, Lord Wilsford emphasised when writing to Lord Somerset how awful the conditions were in Haddington, East Lothian

---

28   E. Gemmill, *Debt, Distraint, Display and Dead Men's Treasure*, p.364. For a much more comprehensive discussion of Arran's clothing go to Schuessler, Bond, M. *Dressing the Scottish Court, 1543–1553: Clothing in the Accounts of the Lord High Treasurer of Scotland,* (Woodbridge, Boydell & Brewer, 2019).

29   1546 TA IX 25.

after the English had taken it in November 1548. He described how the Scots there would 'go in their single white coats, for there is small provision of clothing' (single here being unlined and 'white' meaning undyed wool).[30]

Patten claims 'that vileness of port [dress] was the cause that so many of their great men and gentlemen were killed; and so few saved.' This has always seemed a most unlikely statement given the concerns of the sumptuary laws and the amount of money spent on clothes recorded in the Treasurer's Accounts.[31]

Knee-high or thigh high boots were expensive and therefore were worn by elite men, probably mainly for riding; they were certainly worn by the Regent and the King. King James V has a thigh high pair of boots on in the depiction of him in the Seton Armorial. The Regent's brother had boots and spurs made for him in 1545, (buttis, spurris and sockis), as well as a helmet (a steill bonnet), a jack (ane jack), he also had a winger (quhinger), a short curved sword quite frequently used by the Borderers.[32]

The majority of men wore flat, square-toed shoes. Elite men might have slashing or other decoration on the toes of their shoes but other men simple, plain shoes. Heels on men's shoes came in towards the end of the century.

In 1575 Ministers of the Church of Scotland, were warned against the use of bright colours and luxurious fabrics in their dress. It might have been expected that if, as in England, fine knitted stockings were coming into general use, the evils of wearing them would have been mentioned, but, interestingly enough, strictures about legwear are limited to 'all kynd of superfluitie of cloath in makeing of hose.' This strongly suggests that although knitted hats, sleeves (although these were really for women and children at this period) and vests were definitely around, knitted stockings had not yet become popular in Scotland.[33]

The earliest likely date for knitted stockings in Scotland is the 1580s. There are then 'iij payr of fyne knyt stockings'[34], however they remained unpopular until the 17th century and even then cloth stockings were the mainstay of Highland clothing and stocking frame stockings did not become popular or commonplace in Scotland, the way they had in England, until the latter part of the 18th century despite several attempts.

During the 16th century, the number of gunners at Edinburgh Castle rose to approximately 26 men.[35] Patten says that the Earl of Huntly had 'four or five pieces of ordnance on his right side at Pinkie, and four thousand

---

30 J. Bain, J et al (Eds), *Calendar of State Papers, Scotland: 1547–1603*, (London: Her Majesty's Stationery Office 1898). British History Online, http://www.british-history.ac.uk/cal-state-papers/scotland/ Volume 1 p.166.
31 W. Patten, 'The Expedition into Scotland', p.127.
32 1545 TA VIII 371
33 *Book of the Universall Kirk of Scotland*, (Edinburgh, Maitland Club, 1839), p.149.
34 "Knit *ppl. adj.*". *Dictionary of the Scots Language*. 2004. Scottish Language Dictionaries Ltd. Accessed 19 November 2022.
35 D. Caldwell, 'Edinburgh Castle's Role as a Gun House'.

horsemen on his left.'[36] Gun making had continued at the castle – in 1539 £4 10s (*ane grete mast to be patrouis*) to make the gun-moulds with and 5s for it to be brought from Leith to the castle. These are wooden moulds that were used for casting bronze guns.

In the winter of 1570/1 in the last stages of the Marian civil war, Chisholm, the comptroller of the artillery and a Marian loyalist, was sent to France to obtain money and arms. However when he returned to Scotland in June he was captured by Lord Lindsay and taken to the Regent's camp at Leith. He had about 6,000 francs in cash and on board his ship were 12 barrels of serpentine powder for priming guns, 100 bullets for cannon, 300 bullets for smaller pieces, 300 calivers, 300 morions and 200 pikes.[37]

In 1571, the Regent Lennox attempted to attack Edinburgh Castle, the major centre for Marian loyalists after the fall of Dumbarton Castle. He brought three guns that he put into an earthwork fortification or gun position on Carlton Hill, now just at the end of Princes Street.

A new attempt was made in the autumn by the Regent Mar, who gathered together ten battering pieces, including two from Dumbarton, two from Stirling, one from Dundee, two from Broughty Craig and the other three from Dunbar and elsewhere. Two guns were placed on Salisbury Crags on 10 October but one of them broke the same day,[38] and the Regent's tent was torn by shot.[39] In the winter the English came to support the Regent and brought, among their cannon 'ane Scottis peice les nor ane cannoun, quhilk was tane be the Inglismen at the field of Flodane; she wes callit ane of the sevin sistaris.'[40] By May 1573 all the large artillery in the Castle was out of action in one way or another.

The Castle (and by extension the Royal Artillery) received some new guns in the 1590s from the

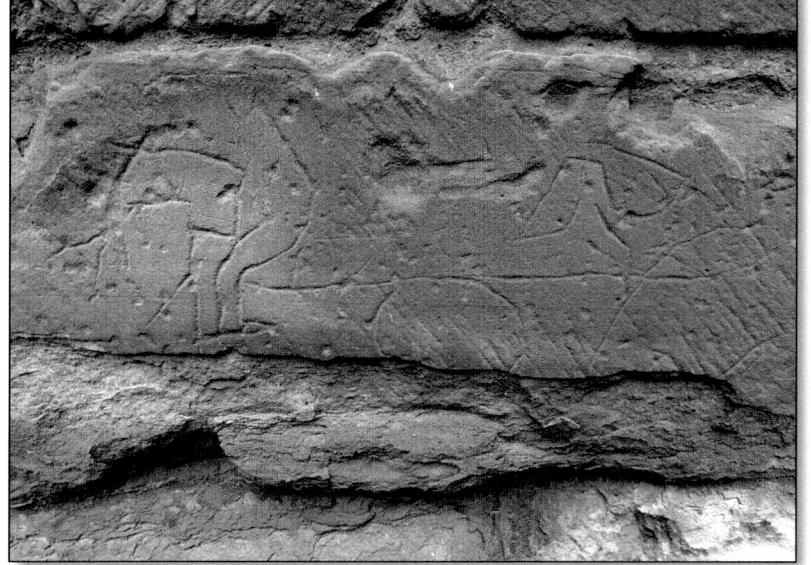

Graffiti of a cannon at the siege of Haddington, from St Mary's Church. (© Sean Chamberlain)

---

36   W. Patten, 'The Expedition into Scotland in 1547', in *Tudor Tracts*. (London, A Constable, 1903), p.113.

37   D. H. Caldwell, 'Edinburgh Castle Under Siege,1559–1573', *Journal of the Sydney Society for Scottish History*, Volume 17, 2018 (Sydney 2018), pp.18–19.

38   D. H. Caldwell, 'Edinburgh Castle Under Siege,1559–1573', *Journal of the Sydney Society for Scottish History*, Volume 17, 2018 (Sydney 2018), p.21.

39   *Bannatyne's Memorials*, pp.192 & 194–5. *Diurnal*, pp.251–2.

40   D. H. Caldwell, 'Edinburgh Castle Under Siege,' p.24 footnote.

Spanish Armada. The first gun to arrive in Scotland was a massive cannon, either a 36-pdr or a 40-pdr, emblazoned with a new Latin inscription, which proudly proclaimed it as a gift from the Lord of Dunluce, James MacDonald, to the King of Scotland. In exchange, the King gave him a knighthood, a vast lordship in Kintyre and a tour of the artillery defences of Edinburgh Castle (on 4 April 1597), where the gun itself was eventually installed.

Patten describes the Scots Army at Pinkie as:

> all well furnish with jack and skull[helmet] dagger, buckler, and swords all notably broad and thin, of exceeding good temper and universally so made to slice, that as I never saw any so good, so think I it hard to devise the better. Hereto, every man his pike ; and a great kercher wrapped twice or thrice about his neck; not for cold but for cutting.[41]

There had been a relatively large investment in munitions grade armour.[42] Mary of Guise, James V's wife sent for a French armourer in 1538. James certainly had armour made for him by a French armourer, 'Jacques' who made the King a suit with tassets and a steel bonnet. The King bought stands of fashionable French armour before he married his first wife.[43] His armour was lined 'Deliverit to Guilliame, armorar, to lyn the Kingis harnes, iij elnis dome grane.' The King also had a royal jack maker, 'Ane lettre maid to Johnne Clerk, mak and him principale jak-makkar to oure soverane lord.'[44]

In 1541, 50 harnesses with mail pissantes [a mail collar or standard], 'fyfty pare of harnes, all witht pissantis of malȝe.'[45] It is difficult to know exactly what a pair of harness was but the likelihood is that it was at least a back and breast plate. Obviously 50 would not provide for the army since men were, according to the legislation, expected to provide their own, but it would go some way to providing for many in the King's household.

The shape of armour had changed during the 16th century and mimicked the fashionable clothes that its owners wore, thus in the early part of the century it was square and bulky, much like the clothes, with the toes for the sabatons flat like the shoes of the period. However, towards the middle and end of the century the waist on armours dropped and became more pronounced, until eventually in the 1570s it is possible to see an echo of the fashionable peascod belly.

---

41   W. Patten, 'The Expedition into Scotland', p.112.
42   1541 TA VII 124
43   1538 TA VII 13
44   Jak *n.2*". *Dictionary of the Scots Language*. 2004. Scottish Language Dictionaries Ltd. Accessed 30 Jun 2022.
45   1541/2 TA VII 123

THE MEN OF WARRE

Detail of statue of James V on Northeast corner of The Royal Palace, Stirling Castle. (© RCAMHS)

Armour was frequently lined and often covered with fabric, but there is no evidence that armour in Scotland was painted. Patten also says that the Scots were all clad alike in jacks covered with white leather; 'doublets of the same or of fustian [fustian was certainly a very common choice, leather far less so]; and most [were wearing] commonly all white hosen.'[46] White hose were popular with the Scots for wearing with armour.

Patten also suggests that many of the men were not wearing armour. It is likely that the majority of the Highlanders were not heavily armoured, most wearing mail or a jack since they were archers. Highlanders customarily did not wear a great deal of armour but it seems unlikely that the gentlemen amongst them would not have been wearing armour. Many men are likely to have worn livery coats with a saltire on them, James V had popularised the use of the thistle imagery. There are at least two portraits and one coin with him wearing a thistle livery collar. Those men who were part of a feudal levy rather than with the common army may well also have worn a badge of the lord who raised them or whose household they were a part of, for example the heart badge of the Douglases.

There were musicians to sound commands on the field, 'foure trumpetoures quha past furtht [out] with the army.'[47] Most of the men would have been wearing jacks, padded linen armour, some with chains along the arms to turn back sword blows, or perhaps a breastplate to deflect blows from halberd or pike, and a helmet, often a plain knapscull with a bonnet on top and some padding underneath. For elite men, the helmet shape had changed post Pinkie to the morion *with a long coxcomb*. These men often had helmets that were gilded and lined with velvet, 'Ane giltin murione'.[48]

---

46 Patten, W. 'The Expedition into Scotland p116
47 1547 TA IX 113.
48 1565 TA XI 455.

86

In 1523, 1545 and 1572, burghs were required to supply food to the army 'on ane competent price,' and officials on royal estates were to provide carriage horses and men to transport these supplies.[49] This was unusual, normally Scots royal armies were expected to forage for themselves.

As in previous battles, the army at Pinkie had banners displaying religious iconography. The banner known as the 'Fetternear Banner' was once thought to be one such, however, it appears to be from a Confraternity of the Holy Blood, and have been used in Guild processions.[50] Patten describes a banner of the 'Kirkmen'; A banner of white sarsenet [a form of taffeta] 'a woman, with her hair about her shoulders, kneeling before a crucifix; and on her right hand, a church.'[51]

The Marchmont banner, a banner of the Home family, has survived and is now in the collection of the National Museum of Scotland – judging from the script and embroidery it appears likely to have been carried on the field at Pinkie.

In 1548, a red and yellow standard (the royal livery colours) was made from silk, a red spear was made for it and the painter paid for painting the banner, 'ane speir to this standart.' The next entry records the making of a red and yellow ensign that required nine ells of taffeta, and it had four ells of 'quhite taffate' to make a cross on it.[52]

In April 1548, Haddington, a royal burgh 20 miles (32 kilometres) from Edinburgh was captured by Lord Gray. He fortified the town and the long siege of Haddington began. At the siege of Haddington, Jean de Beaugué said:

> several savages followed them and they were naked except their stained [presumably yellow] shirts, and a certain light covering made of wool of various colours [this could be tartan], carrying large bows and similar swords and bucklers to the others.

The French original says 'grand arcs' which in this context can be taken to mean long bows as opposed to crossbows. As would be expected from Highlanders at this era they are almost certainly bareheaded. 'Naked' in this context does not actually mean literally naked, simply without the several layers of clothing that the writer considers to be appropriate and 'normal'.

Lowland Scots had not really taken to the long bow except for hunting and sport despite repeated attempts on the part of the monarchy to legislate to the contrary. Similarly unsuccessful had been the attempts to

---

49 D. Caldwell, *The Defence of the Scottish Border*, p.74.
50 Rev. D. MacDonald, 'The Fetternear Banner', *Innes Review*, Volume 7, Issue 2 (Edinburgh, Edinburgh University Press 1956), pp.69–87.
51 W. Patten, 'The Expedition into Scotland', p.132. J. Cooper, *Scottish Renaissance Armies: 1513–1550* (Oxford, Osprey, 2008), p.80, suggests that this could have been from the Abbot of Dunfermline's retinue.
52 1548 TA IX 177.

create a heavy cavalry and since the end of the 15th century the import of horses from England had been banned. An early act of 1424 stated that all gentlemen with an income of more than £20 Scots should have a suitable horse 'as a gentleman ought to',[53] but these gentlemen had failed to rise to this challenge. James V sought to improve the nation's breeding stock by importing horses from Denmark but this did not really make an impact until the latter part of the century.

---

53   Quoted in M. Hayward, 'Outlandish Superfluities…', p.117.

8

Uncivil kind of clothes

> Purge your country piece by piece from vnciwill kind of clothes, such as plaids, mantels, truses and blew bonnets… Cause the inhabitants of the country to cloith them selfs as the civil provinces of the kingdome with doublet, hoise, cloiks and hats [1]

The chief's core retinue seems to have been 12 men, a bodyguard (Luchdtighe). Martin says 'a competent number of young gentlemen called luchttaeh or guard de corps who always attended the chieftain at home or abroad.'[2] The warrior elite in latter part of the 16th century were still largely expected not to work the land:

> in raising or furthbringing of thair men ony time of year to quhat sumevir cuntrie or weiris, na labourer of the ground are permittit to steir forth of the cuntrie quhatevir thair maister have ado, except only gentlemen quhilk labouris not, that the labour belong to the teiling of the ground and wynning of thair corns may not be left undone.[3]

The typical battle sequence was charge, engage, and pursue or in adverse circumstances run away. However, in the mid 16th century this not what the Highlanders were used for. At Pinkie they did not advance to contact; they were routed early in the battle when they came under fire from English ships. The bows carried by these troops provide the greatest clue to their battlefield tactics.

---

1 Sir W. Fraser, *The Sutherland Book* (Edinburgh, T. & A. Constable, 1892.) II, p.359.
2 M. Martin, *A Description of the Western Islands*, p.167.
3 D. Rixson, *The West Highland Galley*, p.57.

> Since the invention of Guns, they are very early accustomed to use them, and carry their pieces with them wherever they go. They likewise learn to handle the broad sword and Target. The Chief of each tribe advances with his followers within shot of the enemy, having first set aside their upper Garments; and after one General discharge, they attack them with sword in hand, having their Target on their Hand'[4]

As Martin makes clear, they carried a gun or other projectile weapon – spear, bow and arrows and a sword. Although he is incorrect about the idea of early adoption of the gun as it took some while for the gun to become embedded in Highland culture. Aonghas MacDonald fought his son in 1598, he had 'his swerd in his hand with his targe, and had lykwys ane pistoilet in his other hand.'[5] Glenlivet in 1594 involved guns and its outcome was at least partially affected by the volley of gunfire at the start:

> Errol and Auchindoun with hundred horsemen charged the shot, killing some of them. The field pieces also playing on them, many fled…many, with the advantage of some bushes near the place of the encounter, stood and poured such a volley of bullets and shower of arrows on the horsemen and horses that Auchindoun and other gentlemen of the Gordons with the most part of horses were slain.

In the early part of the 16th century, the two-handed West Highland claymore was likely to have been a badge of rank used by the Highland aristocracy, with the most common weapon being the two-handed axe. However, by the middle of the century, the two-handed axe in its traditional form was less of a feature in the West Highland armoury. In 1545, a large force of Scots in Ireland was described as being armed with 'long swords and long bows and few guns'. Whereas, later in the century the increased obtainability of the swords meant that the claymore became the weapon of choice for those who could afford it, although the axe, a less expensive weapon to make and obtain, continued in some places, however it became less common. The two-handed axe retained a place and evolved in the Highlands, in name at least, into the Lochaber Axe, the earliest mention of which is in 1500.[6] Elsewhere there were very similar looking axes or polearms that were used in the 16th century, for example the Jedward Stave or the Leith Axe.[7] 'The

---

[4] M. Martin, *A Description of the Western Islands*, p.210.
[5] M. MacGregor, *Warfare in Gaelic Scotland*, quoted on p.225.
[6] For ane batale ax maid of Lochabir fasoun 1500 TA II 111
[7] T. Willis, 'The Scottish Two Handed Sword', *ASAC Bulletin*, volume 120, September 2019, p.51. Note that in the quote the bows are described as 'long bows'. Is this because it is unusual and they would normally have had short bows or simply because it's more menacing?

Gordons were well equipped for the fray, being armed with] bowis, swordis, targes, lochquhaber axis, hagbutis and pistolettis'.[8] However, there are other clan battles around this time that guns appear to have played no part in. It was a combination of arrows and musket fire that made the battle of Glenlivet in 1594 different.

In most circumstances, the typical battle sequence was charge, engage, and pursue or in adverse circumstances run away. Accounts of the battle of Traigh Ghruinneart, Islay fought between the MacDonalds and Macleans in 1598 have Sir Lachlan Maclean killed by an arrow.[9] Reports written at the end of the 16th century about the numbers of men the West Highland chiefs could call suggest that only one-third or approximately 2,000 men were equipped with 'attounes' (aketons) and 'haberchounis' (haubergeons), and 'knapshal bannets' (bascinets)[10] In April 1594, the MacDonalds were sent £300 in 'silver and silver work' with the promise of another £600, half of which was to be paid in armour, clothes, and horses, when they landed in Ireland.[11] By the end of the century guns were on their way to becoming more prevalent despite the key importance of the sword in Highland culture.

Bagpipes are often thought of as being quintessentially Highland and therefore having been around in Highland warfare since time immemorial. However in a form anything like the great pipes of today they were only introduced onto the battlefield in the 16th century. It seems likely that there were bagpipers with Argyll's Highland archers at the disastrous battle of Pinkie Cleugh in 1547 as well as at the siege of Haddington, where Jean de Beaugué describes a piper as being present.[12]

Highlanders were perfectly aware of fashion elsewhere, for example in a contemporary song which dates from 1600. *Bothan Airigh am Braigh Raithneach* (The Shieling in the Braes of Rannoch) a girl goes through a sort of shopping list to her lover. Her 'beautiful gloves and golden ears of corn on their finger-tips.' By this, she means the long fingered high fashion gloves of the late Elizabethan period, which would have been available to her boyfriend in Perth or Edinburgh if he had enough money.[13] However as the quote at opening of the chapter makes clear, the elite men in the

---

8   Lochaber-ax *n.*". *Dictionary of the Scots Language*. 2004. Scottish Language Dictionaries Ltd. Accessed 1 Dec 2021
9   T. Caldwell, 'Having the Right Kit', p.164.
10 R. M. Crawford, *Warfare in the West Highlands and Isles of Scotland, c. 1544–1615*, (Glasgow, unpublished PhD thesis, 2016) quoted on p.81.
11 R. M. Crawford, *Warfare in the West Highlands and Isles of Scotland, c. 1544–1615*, (Glasgow, unpublished PhD thesis, 2016) quoted on p.70.
12 H. Cheape, *Bagpipes – A National Collection of a National Instrument* (Edinburgh, National Museums of Scotland. 2008).
13 H. Cheape, 'The Ethnology of the Old Ways in Gaelic Scotland', J. Bonehill, J. Dulau A. Beveridge, & N. Leask (Eds) *Old Ways New Roads: Travels in Scotland 1720–1832*, (Edinburgh, Birlin, 2021) p.46.
    I am indebted to Professor Cheape for first bringing the significance of this particular line to my attention in an online talk for the Hunterian.

THE MEN OF WARRE

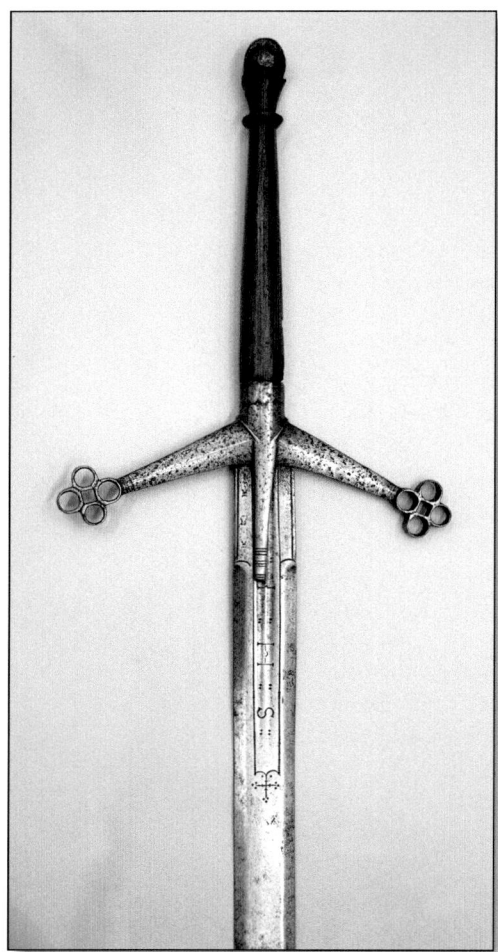

Breadalbane Claymore. This is a rare complete example of the classic form of two-handed sword used in the Highlands. The term is also applied to the basket-hilted sword characteristic of Scotland from at least the eighteenth century onward. (© Metropolitian Museum of Art)

Highlands had for the most part moved away from the saffron coloured shirts, which the Western Highlanders wore in the mid century, poorer men just wore long shirts and towards the clothes that by the 17th century would become more familiar as Highland dress. The poor would have been bare legged and often bare foot. Men on the east coast in general had never worn saffron coloured shirts, although the wearing of a plaid or mantle was common to all areas of the Highlands but only in the West did it tend to be fringed like the Irish ones.

The earliest mention of tartan in an official document is probably a 'tartane galcoit gevin to the king be the Maister Forbes in 1532.' It is of course very difficult to know whether that is anything like the checked, twill fabric that people today would recognise as tartan. Six years later the King had 15 ells of Holland linen for a long Highland shirt (side Hieland sarkis), three ells of Highland tartan for hose, two ells and quarter to make a Highland short coat (variant cullorit velvet to be Kingis grace ane Heland schort coit).[14] This is a glimpse of the clothing of aristocratic Highland men. A long shirt with a huge amount of material in it was a way of demonstrating the elite nature of the garment. At this time, these shirts had voluminous sleeves, which often came to the elbow or just below.

A short coat and tartan hose although these were long hose, this outfit bears a strong resemblance to the drawing by Lucas de Heere from 1568 where the highlander depicted wears short hose, a short coat which might be tartan and a mantle. He carries a claymore, the pommel of which suggests that it is a West Highland claymore, similar to the one held by John Macleod in the effigy at Rodel, Harris.

In the East Highland and Lowland regions, there is little evidence for the intermediate sword types between the swords of 'de Greenlaw' type and the Clamshell and Lowland Claymores. The development sequence is not illustrated in the funerary monuments as is the case for the West Highland claymore. Tradition suggests that the hereditary armourers of the Lords of the Isles were based on Islay.[15] Caldwell further suggests that it is possible

---

14   1538 TA Vi 436
15   D. H. Caldwell, *Islay: The Land of the Lordship,* (Edinburgh, Birlinn, 2008), p.127. Of course in this period most armourers in the medieval and early modern eras were hereditary in that sons tended to go into their father's professions and unfortunately there are very few records for the Highlands at this time for this sort of thing. There were bowyers and armourers working in Inverness in1600.

UNCIVIL KIND OF CLOTHES

that there might be a particular type of sword hilt that could be an Islay hilt, which leaves open the possibility that in the same way that it is possible to identify district or area tartans (because of weaving patterns and styles) it might be possible to do the same for swords.

Jean de Beaugué at the siege of Haddington, in the 1540s described the Highlanders:

> *Ies ont nuz fors que de leurs chemises taintes de certaines couvertures legeres faites de laine, de plusieurs coleurs.*
> [They wear no clothes except their dyed shirts and a sort of light woollen covering of several colours.][16]

Bishop John Leslie in his Historie of Scotland, written in 1578, described clothes that men in the West Highlands were wearing:

> All, both nobles and common people, wore mantles of one sort (except that the nobles preferred those of several colours). These were long and flowing, but capable of being neatly gathered up at pleasure into folds…Wrapped into these for their only covering, they could sleep comfortably…The rest of their garments consisted of a very short woollen jacket with the sleeves open below for the convenience of throwing their darts, and a covering for the thighs of the simplest kind, more for decency than for show or defence against the cold. They made also of linen very large shirts with numerous and wide folds which flowed loosely to their knees. These the rich, coloured with saffron and others smeared with some grease to preserve them clean among the toils and exercise of a camp… In the manufacture of these, ornament and a certain attention to taste were not altogether neglected and they joined the different parts of their shirts very neatly with silk thread, chiefly of a red or green colour.[17]

Although a long Highland shirt in the royal inventory in 1578 was decorated with purple and silver edgings, 'Ane hieland syd [long] serk of yallow lyning [yellow linen] pasmentit with purpour silk and silver.'[18] In the same year in the royal inventory, there was also a Highland mantle, 'Ane hieland mantill of blak freis pasmentit with gold and lynit with blak taffetie.'[19] It is possible

---

16   H. F. McClintock, *Old Irish and Highland Dress*, (Dundalk, Dundalgan Press, 1943), p.112. This quote has been edited slightly to make it easier to read.
17   Ibid., p.114.
18   T. Thomson (ed.), *A Collection of Inventories and other Records of the Royal Wardrobe and Jewel House and of the artillery and munitioun in some of the royal castles, 1488–1606.* (Edinburgh, Bannatyne Club, 1815), p.277.
19   T. Thomson (ed.), *A Collection of Inventories*, p.273. Earlier mantles are often described as Irish

THE MEN OF WARRE

that these were intended for masques rather than as items of everyday wear. Mary, Queen of Scots, had 'wild Highland men' dressed in goatskins at her masques in 1566.[20] However, she wore Highland mantles on several occasions.

The O'Domhnaill chiefs pioneered the use of redshanks, who were recruited from the Isles each summer to fight in Ireland. This use of larger numbers of mercenary soldiers helped to change the nature of warfare in Ireland as it made pitched battles against the English more feasible.[21] During the 16th century the differences between the elite warriors of the chiefs' households and the Galloglass, and the clansmen or redshanks as well as the kern in Ireland, became less marked. In a letter to the English agent Robert Bowes, dated 18 March 1595/6, Lachlan MacLean of Duart on Mull, specifies what he can provide for English service in Ireland in a single raiding season:

A jack of plates, c1560. A sleeveless doublet popular with horsemen, such as those from the Borders, and ordinary soldiers and sailors in Scotland during the sixteenth century. This one takes has the peascod form of the fashionable doublet. The holes are reinforced with wire rings. The jack is made of small overlapping iron plates sewn between the layers of fabric with crossbow twine. (©Royal Armouries).

> 1500 bowmen and 500 fyremen [That is men who could use guns] In this number we will not want our two-handed swords and armour of mail to be used if battle be offered to us; at which time we will change some of our bowmen to use their two-handed swords the time of battle.[22]

This was however, the last hurrah of the mercenary trade across the Irish sea, by the beginning of the next century Argyll was able to effectively crush the Islay uprising in 1615.[23]

---

20 L. Mickel, 'Our Hielandmen', Scots In Court Entertainment at Home and Abroad, p.193.
21 K. Simms, 'From Kings to Warlords', p.126–7.
22 'James VI, August 1595', J. Bain et al (Eds) *Calendar of State Papers, Scotland: Volumes 1, 2, 3, 5, 11 1547–1603* (London, Her Majesty's Stationery Office, 1898). British History Online, http://www.british-history.ac.uk/cal-state-papers/scotland, pp.664–691. [Accessed 9 July 2022].
23 M. MacGregor, *Warfare in Gaelic Scotland in the Later Middle Ages*, p.211.

Colour Plate Commentaries

A. 15th century knight

The Scots lowland knight or man-at-arms of the mid to late 15th century wore armour that to his English counterparts would have looked slightly old-fashioned. Underneath he is wearing long white hose and a silk arming doublet. He is wearing an aventail and a bascinet, the Scots continued to wear this style well into the 15th century. In battle, he would have worn coat armour over his breastplate with his coat of arms or in a livery colour with a badge, which were quite often painted. His belt would often have had similar heraldic devices on it. He is wearing a separate mail skirt; these seem often to have been lined, as were other pieces of armour. His breastplate is hinged on the left and strapped to him on his right. He is carrying an arming sword and has a baselard dagger.

B. Galloglass/Chief

This West Highland clan chief is wearing a bright saffron dyed shirt underneath a long padded linen aketon. He is carrying a hand and half sword, which has an ivory handle and he has an axe in his other hand. The brightness of the shirt was a mark of his status, the majority of the men in the West Highlands did not wear such bright colours or use the extravagant amounts of fabric and dye that these shirts required. He is wearing a bascinet and a mail aventail and a mail shirt or habergeon. Pitscottie described the West Highlanders as 'Airmit ... with haberiunes... and exis.'

C. Soldier at Pinkie

He is wearing a simple knapscull, which would have been padded inside, covered by a blue knitted and felted bonnet. These helmets were commonly covered by such bonnets. He has a woollen kerchief wrapped round his neck, something Patten describes many of the Scots wearing against 'the cutting', white hose and a grey doublet; dress which would have been common amongst lower class men in the army. Over the doublet, but under his white coat, he wears a padded linen jack. He is shown carrying the

'Boswell of Balmuto guidon', which was captured at Pinkie by Sir William Norris.

D. Borderer

This man is wearing a coxcomb morion helmet, a jack of plates, grey doublet, breeches and knee riding length boots with spurs. He is well armed, with an early basket hilt sword, wooden hafted dagger and a pistol. The blades of both sword and dagger are likely to have been imported from Germany and assembled with hilt and guard by a Scottish cutler or swordslipper. The pistol, however, has been made in Scotland, probably Edinburgh or Dundee where there were several pistol or dagmakers.

E. Marian Gunner

Gunners were often given black clothes, reflecting their high status. He is wearing fashionable Venetian black breeches and black woollen short hose held up with garters. He has a breast and back plate and a skullcap covered by a black wool cap. He is carrying gunpowder in a wooden powder flask although separate powder charges were starting to be used, his lead shot is in another bag and his long match is ready to touch the pan when required.

F. Highland Gentleman

He is illustrated as wearing fashionable 16th century armour with a peascod belly and tassets, something generally missing from earlier Scottish armour. However, unlike his counterparts in the south of Scotland or in England he is fighting with the distinctively Highland two-handed claymore. Guns, although popular in the south of Scotland (indeed the first assassination by gun took place in Linlithgow in 1570 of James Stewart, 1st Earl of Moray, the then Regent) did not appear in Highland warfare until the 1590s.

G. Highland Archer

This archer in his yellow shirt and short blue doublet is one of Argyll's men, the size of his sleeves showing his status. This is a highly fashionable garment for the mid 16th century in West Highland society. West Highland men at this time were generally bare headed and customarily wore their hair loose. His arrows may have been fletched with eagle feathers, and his bowstring coated with wax brought from Galway. He would also have had a fringed mantle, which may have been check, which he would have worn like a cloak or pulled over his head in cold or rainy weather, but he has cast this aside for battle.

COLOUR PLATE COMMENTARIES

H. Later Highlander

A poor man, at the end of the 16th century, wearing a rough linen shirt, and a version of the belted plaid in browns and yellows from local dyes. He could pull the plaid over his head if he were cold. Some sources suggest that on cold nights, highlanders might wet the plaid and the body heat of the wearer made it much warmer. Elite and wealthier men wore the plaid with trews, a short doublet or breeches and cloth hose. However, most lower class men wore it with bare legs or short cloth hose and a doublet, the rest of the plaid gathered onto their shoulder with a bodkin of wood, bone or metal depending on social class. A noticeable difference from earlier in the century is that Highlanders were now wearing hats; the blue bonnet had by now become a near ubiquitous indicator of the Scotsman but especially the Highlander. At the end of the 16th century, many of the highlanders still learned to shoot bows although firearms were becoming more common. A Lochaber axe was a cheap and effective weapon for close quarter fighting for many men.

Glossary

Acton, Aketon
A stuffed defensive garment, sometimes worn under mail. The name had originally referred to the stuffing but later came to refer to whole garment The long padded garments worn on the west coast and in the Isles and by Galloglass in particular (see also paltok, jak hogton).

Array
To put into order – clothes, or men into battle order

Arming Doublet
Worn under armour as a foundation garment, to which parts of armour were attached and would act as a buffer when attacked. It was not padded like a jack or an aketon.

Arming Shoes/Shoon
Neatly fitting leather boots worn with harness. Also used to refer to mail foot coverings and sabatons

Arming Sword
Single-handed with a cruciform hilt and a straight and straight double-edged blade of around 69 to 89 centimetres (27 to 35 inches).

Armourer
Originally a maker of defensive armour only, a maker or setter up of any type of arms or armours. Most frequently by the 16th century a mounter of swords. (see also sword slipper)

Aventail
Mail protection for neck and face, attached to a helmet generally lined with material or leather and hung from the lover edge of the bascinet.

Battal Axe (various sorts).
A long shafted axe was one of the common weapons of the Scots soldier in the 15th century.

Bascinet
A helmet with a hinged visor and a mail coif, which seems to have been worn in Scotland more commonly longer than in England.

Baselar, Baselard
A dagger or short sword worn on the belt

Besagew
Small armour plate that protected the armpit.

Bolt
Short, thick arrow for a crossbow.

GLOSSARY

Brayetter, Brayer (see also pance)
Mail breeches for the groin area for men fighting on foot. These were often lined.

Braser
A piece of armour covering the arm. It is important to note that while there may have been several different names for the parts of the armour covering the arm, the names for those, e.g. couter or poleyn, are actually quite rare in medieval texts. Plate slevis; (plate sleeves) also seems to have been used at times.

Breke, Breech
Men's linen under garments and the upper part of hose. In the 16th century, they had become short, often close-fitting worn to the knee, fastening at the front

Brogit/Broggit Staff
A heavy iron head from which spikes projected in all directions, and sometimes with a spearhead.

Bombard
An early cannon, but often used before the 16th century to mean any sort of artillery.

Bowar/Bouer/Bow – maker
In Edinburgh generally a member of the incorporation of wrights rather than a hammerman e.g. a wood worker not a metal worker. He was frequently a supplier of spears, pikes & clubs.

Brigandine
A brigandine, or a pair of brigandines, was a sleeveless jacket, normally laced up the front, in which plates or scales of metal were riveted together beneath a covering of cloth. In Scotland in 1491 the law decreed 'that every man be furnished and equipped in his body with white harness, brigandine tin or good jakkis with plate armour and gauntlets and complete harness, well mounted, corresponding to their lands and goods'.

Broadsword
A sword with a broad, straight two-edged blade. (claidheamh mor or claidheamh leathann).

Buckler
A small round shield made from metal, or sometimes leather

Camlet
Mixed fabric often combining goat hair with wool or silk.

Capiteberne
Hood for a cloak. Hoods by the end of the 15th century were generally worn only for travelling or working. This was a change from early in the century where they had been worn more widely.

Calico, Calicult
Printed cotton, originally from Calcutta, India.

Cassock
A loose coat like gown.

Chammlet, Camlet
Originally an eastern fabric, later a warp faced tabby cloth with a pronounced weft rib. It was imported from Angora and Cyprus.

Chanfron, Shaffron, Chauffron, chafferonis
Horse armour, specifically for the face. Cavalry was an important element of all European armies even the Scots for many centuries. Although striking a horse while jousting was definitely frowned on, it was difficult to prevent it happening during a battle. The horses that they used were smaller than perhaps might be commonly thought. Working horses often being only around 13 hands and warhorses being about 15 hands in the 15th and 16th centuries. Glasgow Museums holds some beautiful examples of horse armour from this period, mostly made in Germany. The barded horses in Albany's army in 1523 would have been wearing this and other armour and indeed later armies there are records of the King's horses having barding in 1542. It could be made from metal or cheaper leather. In 1539, £8 was paid to Thomas Schort for 'iij chafferonis for the grete hors'.

Chape, Crampet
Metal tip of scabbard

Chaperon
A French word used to describe a hood with a cape and liripipe. It was worn between approximately 1420 and 1470 as part of fashionable dress. Although it was part of male dress the word was adopted into Scots and was later used to mean hat and then a woman's hood.

Coat Armour
A surcoat, often with a heraldic device. It used to be thought that since coat armour is not commonly shown on effigies in England after the mid 15th century that it had stopped being worn. In Scotland, it seems likely that the very smooth breastplate that the effigies are generally shown with, demonstrated that they were wearing coat armour. Scots accounts show that they were buying it and wearing it well into the 16th century.

Corselet
A close-fitting garment which protected the body, often used to refer to armour.

Cote, Coat.
Worn over a doublet. Shorter than a gown often worn by lower status men. Sometimes with a badge or other symbol identifying them as part of a household or other employ or in the household colours of their employer. Livery coats were often quartered.

Cross Hilt
The simplest form of hilt for a sword with a guard consisting of a single bar – the quillons

Culmas
A curved sword; a sabre

Culverin
An early form of muzzle loaded handgun firing iron shot There were grosse culverins which had a calibre of $4\frac{2}{3}$in (118mm), demi culverins with a calibre of $4\frac{1}{2}$in (114mm), culverin bastard with a calibre of $3\frac{5}{6}$in

(97mm) and double culverin, moyen/culverin, pikmoyen (the meaning of pikmoyen is not clear). Those had a calibre of 3½ (89mm).

Cutler, Cultellar
A maker of knives and daggers.

Dag
A heavy pistol or handgun.

Dagmaker
A maker of dags or pistols

Dence/Danes Axe
A 'Danish' Axe, a long bladed axe

Dichting
The putting in good order of metal weapons

Ell
A measure of cloth. By an Act of Parliament of 1427, Scots ell was regulated as 37 inches.

Fleggearis, Fletcher
A maker of arrows.

Fustian
Imported from Ulm in Germany or from Naples, some also came from England, linen warp and cotton weft. It had a short even nap that hid the weave. Cotton was imported from the east at this period.

Gairdmaker
A maker of sword guards. There were several types of sword guards in the 16th century.

Galbart, Garbadine
Riding coat.

Gantillet, Gantle
A gauntlet. This word seems to have been used as opposed to gluffis from the middle of the 16th century although they do seem to have been called gauntlet gloves (gantillet gluif).

Gorget
Worn under the cuirass and intended to cover a larger area of the neck, shoulders and upper chest. The gorget served as an anchor point for the pauldrons, which either had holes in them to engage pins projecting from the gorget, or straps which could be buckled to the gorget.

Gluvis/Gluffis of Plait
Gauntlets. Leather gloves were worn while riding, hunting and shooting. They were often ordered in multiple pairs. Mittens might be knitted or made from cloth.

Gunner
Used both as a man who fires guns and a maker of guns.

Habergeon, Haubergeon (see also aketon, hogton, jack and paltok)
A sleeveless coat or jacket, of mail or leather, worn as a piece of body armour.

Hackbut, Hagbut
The word, derived from the Dutch word *Haakbus* - meaning hook gun. Seems to have been used to describe the men who made them sometimes as well. They could be muzzle or breech loading.

Halberd, Halbert
A two-handed pole weapon used during the 14th, fifteenth, and 16th centuries. Troops that used the weapon were sometimes called halberdiers. It generally had a staff. A head with an axe, a central spike and a hook

Hacrek, Halcret
A half-suit of light plate armour, worn alike by footmen and horsemen, with long tassets in the 16th century.

Harden
Coarse, heavyweight linen often used for bags, sacks and shirts for poorer people.

Harnes, Harness (see also harnes mill)
The armour worn by a fighting man.

Harnes mill
The workshop of an armourer (see harness)

Heft, Heftmaker
Someone who made the blades of knives. Seems to have been the same or similar as a cutler.

Hilt (see also sword slipper)
By the end of the 16th century several types of hilt are mentioned in the records.

Hinger, Hanger
It was originally a device by which anything may be hung so there were hangers for arrows and swords.

Hobelar
A lightly armoured man who fought on horseback, used mostly about the Borderers.

Hogton (see aketon, jack and paltok)
A sleeveless padded jerkin worn under a mail shirt, and occasionally alone as a fencing doublet.

Holland
High quality linen cloth. Often used for making shirts (sarks) for elite men.

Hose/Hois
A close-fitting garment for the leg; a stocking, short or long from the feet to the waist or hips,. Until the latter part of the 16th century they were cut from cloth on the bias. At the end of 16th century knitted hose/stockings started to become popular, the earliest confirmed knitted hose in Scotland were in 1583, knitted short hose were not worn with Highland dress.

Jak, Jack (see also aketon, hogton and paltok)
A jerkin or a doublet of defence, generally with sleeves. These followed fashion in their shape. It was usually made from many layers of linen, often stuffed with rags, sometimes lined with leather or for elite men silk and in the 16th century. sometimes with iron plates or cheaper horn.

Jedwart/Jedburgh Stave or staff
A glaive with a narrow four-foot blade mounted on a stave often used by Boderers. 1506, the royal cutler, Robert Selkirk made the King with a 'Jedwort hede' which was gilded.

GLOSSARY

Journe(e), Journa(y), Jurnay,
A kind of cloak worn over the armour, when travelling it was probably decorative.

Kelt
Homespun, grey or black, made from the grey and black fleece of the sheep undyed. A coarse cloth was generally used for outer garments

Kendal
A rough frieze from Kendal in Cumbria used for doublets and coats.

Kersey
Cloth with a 2:2 twill weave which made it ideal for hose when cut on the bias.

Knapscall
Close-fitting metal helmet often worn with a bonnet over the helmet called a Knapscall-bonnet

Knok, Nok, Nock
A small notched piece of horn at the end of a bow. Or a notched piece of horn fixed in the end of an arrow. A notch in either of these or in a crossbow, for holding or receiving the bowstring. Seems also sometimes to have been used to refer to the bow itself.

Lance
Generally refers to a horseman's lance but sometimes a spear. Until the first half of the 15th century (just before the time this book is concerned with) the war lance was normally comprised of a shaft of a tough wood, such as ash, and about 14 foot long (approximately 4.25 metres) with a small steel leaf-shaped head. Frequently, from as early as the beginning of the 14th century a circular steel hand-defence (vamplate), was sometimes fitted over the shaft, but this was more usual on the jousting lance until the second half of the 15th century. It is difficult to find a contemporary Scottish reference to men using them on horseback on the field outwith the Borders except for tourneys.

Latten
Brass or bronze used on effigies and decorative edges on armour
Patten describes the Scots at Pinkie as using 'chains of latten' set along the sleeves and thighs.

Livery
Food, clothing/cloth to make clothing (this was more common for women) or money given to retainers or servants or distinctive clothing to mark a retinue.

Lorimer
A maker of bits, buckles, stirrup irons, other metal parts of a horse's harness, stirrups also spurs and arrowheads. Towards the end of the 16th century at least one lorimer from Edinburgh was described as a dagmaker

Mantil, Mantle
A long robe, open at the waist or a length of fabric worn round the shoulders by the Highlanders/Islesmen in the 15th and early 16th century.

Mell
A heavy hammer or mace, as a weapon of war

Pance, Pans
Mail breeches for the groin and worn under other armour. These were sometimes lined (see also brayette)

Plaid
Length of cloth worn mostly as a garment in a twilled weave, sometimes but not always tartan. Used chiefly as a garment by women throughout Scotland and by men as a mantle or in the Highlands only, as the belted plaid at the end of the 16th century.

Pisane, Pissan
A separate mail collar sometimes worn under the helmet as additional protection.

Point
Sometimes called horning. Metal tag on the end of a lace used to attach hose to a doublet, pieces of armour together, lace shoes together and so on. Laces were generally hemp, linen or sometimes silk.

Plummet
Pommel

Poke/pock
A bag or small sack.

Quarrel
A short, square-headed crossbow bolt or arrow.

Rissilis, Russel
Rijssel was the Flemish name for Lille so the fabric originally at least came from Lille. A woollen cloth of a plain weave

Rullion, Rilling
A raw hide shoe or boot worn by highlanders and islesmen

Russet
Rough wool cloth, often but not always brown-red. Thus it was possible to have green russet.

Saker
Smaller than a demi-culverin, often used in sieges and on ships

Scarlet
A rich cloth, of various colours, often bright red. Up to the Spanish colonisation of the Americas red came from madder or tiny insects 'kermes' which looked liked little grains of wheat. Cochineal, another insect from South America (which gave the bright reds of the 17th century tartans) was much better but not available in Scotland till very late 16th century, more probably the beginning of the 17th century.

Splentis/splints
A piece of armour, chiefly for the arms and legs, probably only protecting the outer part of the arm. In 1547, the King had some which were covered in velvet however they were in general worn by ordinary men.

Bibliography

Primary Sources

Bain, J (Ed), T*he Hamilton Papers : Letters and Papers Illustrating the Political Relations of England and Scotland in the XVIth Century formerly in the Possession of the Dukes of Hamilton, now in the British Museum*, 2 Volumes, (Edinburgh, H.M. General Register House, 1890–92).

Bain, J et al (Ed), *Calendar of State Papers, Scotland: Volumes 1, 2, 3, 5, 11, 1547–1603.* (London, Her Majesty's Stationery Office 1898). British History Online, http://www.british-history.ac.uk/cal-state-papers/scotland/

Beveridge, J. and Russell, J. (eds), *Protocol Books of Dominus Thomas Johnsoun, 1528–78*, (Edinburgh, Scottish Record Society, 1920).

Brown, J. S. K. M. et al (Eds), *The Records of the Parliaments of Scotland to 1707*, (St Andrews, 2007–2021).

Brewer, J. S. (ed.), *Letters and Papers, Foreign and Domestic, Henry VIII, Volume 1, 1509–1514, Volume 3, 1519–1523, Volume 4, 1524–1530.* (London, University of London & History of Parliament Trust, 1920).

Burnett, G., Stuart J. et al (Eds), '*Rotuli Scaccarii Regum Scotorum. The Exchequer Rolls of Scotland*', 22 volumes, 1264–1600. (Edinburgh, H.M. General Register House, 1878–1908).

Burton, J. H. et al (eds) '*Register of the Privy Council of Scotland* [1545–1691]', 16 volumes (Edinburgh, H.M. Register House, 1877–1970).

Calendar of State Papers Domestic, Volumes 1, 2, 3, 7, 8, 11.

Cameron, A., Macbain, A., Kennedy, J., 'The Book of Clanranald' in *Reliquiae Celticae*, Ed. Alexander Macbain, M. A. and Rev. Kennedy. J, (Inverness, The Northern Counties Newspaper and Printing and Publishing Company, Limited 1894) volume 2, pp.149–288.

Cameron, K., Cameron, A., & Kennedy, J., *Reliquiae Celticae : Texts, Papers, and Studies in Gaelic Literature and Philology Left by the Late Rev. Cameron, LL.D.* (Inverness: the Northern Counties Newspaper and Printing and Publishing Company, Limited 1892).

Campbell, D., *The book of Garth and Fortingall : Historical Sketches Relating to the Districts of Garth, Fortingall, Athole, and Breadalbane.* (Inverness,

Chalmers, R, (ed.), *Domestic Annals of Scotland Volume 1, Reign of Mary 1561–1567* (Edinburgh W. Chambers, 1861).

Cody, E. G., Leslie, John, & Murison, W., *The Historie of Scotland*. (Edinburgh: W. Blackwood & Sons for the Scottish History Society, 1888).

Cheape, H. 'The Ethnology of the Old Ways in Gaelic Scotland', J. Bonehill, J. Dulau A. Beveridge, & N. Leask (Eds) *Old Ways New Roads: Travels in Scotland 1720–1832*, (Edinburgh, Birlin, 2021)

Church of Scotland. General Assembly, Peterkin, A., *The Booke of the Universall Kirk of Scotland: Wherein the Headis And Conclusionis Devysit Be the Ministers And Commissionaris of the Particular Kirks Thereof, Are Especially Expressed And Contained.* (Edinburgh, The Edinburgh printing & publishing co., 1839).

Craigie, Sir W., Aitken A. J., Stevenson J. A. C., Watson, H. D. and Dareau, M. G. (eds), *A Dictionary of the Older Scottish Tongue*, (Chicago, Edinburgh, Aberdeen and Oxford 1931, 2002) 12 volumes. online edition, n.d., http://dsl.ac.uk

Crammond, W., *The Annals of Banff*, (Aberdeen, New Spalding Club, 1891) 2 volumes.

Dickson, T., (Ed.), Treasurers' Accounts. *Compota thesaurariorum Regum Scotorum*, (Edinburgh, H. M. General Register House, 1877).

Duncan, W. J., (ed.), *Miscellaneous papers principally illustrative of events in the reigns of Queen Mary and James VI* (Glasgow, Maitland Club, 1834).

Edinburgh Testaments, 1514–32, 1567–1700 MS NAS CC8/8/1–80, 80 vols.

Everett, M, (ed.), *Calendar of State Papers Domestic, Volumes 3, 7, 8*, (London, Longman & Co, 1880–85).

Ferguson, J. & J. (Eds), *Papers Illustrating the History of the Scots Brigade in the Service of the United Netherlands, 1572–1782.* (Edinburgh: T. and A. Constable for the Scottish History Society, 1899).

Fraser, J., (Mackay, W. ed.), *Chronicles of the Frasers: The Wardlaw Manuscript*, (Edinburgh, T. and A. Constable for the Scottish History Society, 1905).

Gregory, D, *The History of the Western Highlands and Isles of Scotland* (Glasgow, W. Tait, 1836).

Harrison. J, *Stirling Castle Palace: Archaeological and Historical Research 2004–2008, The Wardrobe Inventories of James V* (Edinburgh: Kirkdale Archaeology / Historic Scotland 2008).

Hodge, A., *Edinburgh Castle: The Medieval Documents* (Edinburgh, Historic Scotland, 2018).

Holinshed, R., *Holinshed's Chronicles of England, Scotland and Ireland, Vol. 5*, (London, J. Johnson, 1807–08).

Hume-Brown, P. (ed.), *Early Travellers in Scotland* (Edinburgh, Nell & Co, 1891).

Lindsay of Piscottie. R. (E. J. G. Mackay, ed.), *The Historie and Chronicles of Scotland*, 3 volumes (Edinburgh, Scottish Text Society, 1899–1911).

Lemon, R. (ed.), *Calendar of State Papers Domestic, Volumes 1 & 2* (London, Longman & Roberts, 1856).

Mackay, A., *The Book of Mackay,* (Edinburgh, Norman MacLeod, 1906).

Malcolm-Davies, J. & Mikhalia,N. *The Typical Tudor: Reconstructing Everyday 16th Century Dress*, (Lightwater, Fat Goose Press, 2022)

Major, J., (Constable, A. ed.), *A History of Greater Britain as well England as Scotland* (Edinburgh, Scottish History Society, 1892)

Martin. M., *A Description of the Western Islands of Scotland* (Edinburgh, The Mercat Press, 1982).

Marwick, J. D. (ed.), *Records of the Burgh of Edinburgh, 1528–1557*, (Edinburgh, Scottish Burgh Records Society, 1871), *British History Online* http://www.british-history.ac.uk/edinburgh-burgh-records/1528–57

Miscellany of the Maitland Club, consisting of original papers and other documents illustrative of the history and literature of Scotland (Glasgow Maitland Club,, 1840–47).

Patten, W., 'The Expedition into Scotland in 1547', in *Tudor Tracts*. (London, A Constable, 1903).

Paton J. Imrie and Dunbar, J. G. (Eds), *Accounts of the Masters of Works*, 1529 (Edinburgh, H.M. Stationery Office, 1967).

Stavert, M. L. (ed.), *Perth Guildry, The Perth Guildry Book 1452 1601*, 19 (Edinburgh Scottish Records Society,1993).

Taylor, J., (Chandler, John ed.), *Travels Through Stuart Britain: The Adventures of John Taylor, the Water Poet,* (Stroud, Sutton, 1999).

Thomas, A. *Princelie Majestie: The Court of James V of Scotland, 1528–1542* (Edinburgh, John Donald, 2005) Thomson, T. (ed.), *A Collection of Inventories and other Records of the Royal Wardrobe and Jewelhouse and of the artillery and munitioun in some of the royal castles, 1488–1606.* (Edinburgh, Bannatyne Club, 1815).

Thomson, T. (ed.), *Diurnal of the remarkable occurents that have passed within the country of Scotland since the death of James the Fourth till the year MDLXXV* (Bannatyre Club, 1833).

Stevenson, T., *Collectanea de Rebus Albanicis: Consisting of Original Papers and Documents Relating to the History of the Highlands and Islands of Scotland* (Edinburgh, Iona Club, 1847).

Stuart, J., *The Miscellany of the Spalding Club*. (Edinburgh: Spalding Club, 1841.)

Secondary Sources: Books

Anderson, C. & Fleet, C., *Scotland Defending the Nation: Mapping the Military Landscape* (Edinburgh, Birlinn, 2018).

Caldwell. D. H., *Islay: The Land of the Lordship,* (Edinburgh, Birlinn, 2008).

Caldwell. D. H., 'Some Notes on Scottish Shafted Weapons', Caldwell, D. (Ed.), *Scottish Weapons and Fortifications*, (Edinburgh, John Donald, 1981).

Caldwell. D. H., 'The Scots and Guns', King, A. and Penman, M. A. (Eds), *England and Scotland in the Fourteenth Century, New Perspectives*, (Woodbridge, Edinburgh University Press. 2007).

Caldwell. D. H., 'Royal Patronage of Arms and Armour Making in Fifteenth and Sixteenth Century Scotland', Caldwell, D. (ed.), *Scottish Weapons and Fortifications* (Edinburgh, John Donald, 1981).

Caldwell, D. H., 'Having the Right Kit: West Highlanders', Duffy, S (ed.), T*he World of the Galloglass: Kings, Warlords and Warriors in Ireland and Scotland 1200–1600*, (Dublin, Four Courts Press, 2007, 2016) pp.144–168.

Caldwell, D., *Edinburgh Castle's Role as a Gun House*, (Edinburgh, Historic Environment Scotland, 2018).

Campbell of Airds, A. 'West Highland Heraldry and The Lordship of the Isles', *The Lordship of the Isles*, R, Oram (Ed.) (Leiden, Brill, 2014) pp.200–10.

Cannan, F., *Galloglass 1250–1600: Gaelic Mercenary Warrior*, (Oxford, Osprey, 2010).

Capwell, T., *Armour of an English Knight 1450–1500*, (London, Thomas Del Mar Ltd, 2021).

Cathcart, A., 'A Spent Force? : The Clan Donald in the Aftermath of 1493', in *The Lordship of the Isles,* Richard Oram (ed.), (Leiden, 2014), pp.254–7.

Cheape, H., *Bagpipes – A National Collection of a National Instrument*, (Edinburgh, National Museums of Scotland, 2008).

Cheape, H. & Grant, I. F., *Periods in the Highland History*, (Edinburgh, Barnes & Noble, 2000).

Conway, A. *Henry VII's relations with Scotland and Ireland 1485–98,* (Cambridge, Cambridge University Press, 1932).

Christiansen, Carol, and Gabra-Sanders, Thea, 'The Textiles', (Scottish Archaeological Internet Reports 8,1 December 2018), pp.15–47.

Cooper, J., 'What's missing here? Homing in on Haddington's lost defences', *Journal of Conflict Archaeology*, vol. 5, no. 1, 2009, pp.141–62.

Cooper. J., *Scottish Renaissance Armies, 1513–1550*, (Oxford, Osprey, 2008).

Crang, J. A., Spiers, E. M. & Strickland, M. J. (Eds), *A Military History of Scotland*, (Edinburgh, Edinburgh University Press, 2014).

Crawford, B. 'Two Seals from Orkney: The 15th Century Community Seal and a Seal Matrix Dating to c. AD 1300', *Nordic Middle Ages – Artefacts, Landscapes and Society. Essays in Honour of Ingvild Øye on her 70th Birthday,* (Bergen, University of Bergen, 2015) pp.105–117.

Crowfoot, E., Pritchard, F., and Staniland, K., *Textiles and Clothing c.1150-c.1450, Medieval Finds from Excavations in London 4* (London: 1992).

Dean, L. H. S & Buchanan, K. (eds), *Medieval and Early Modern Representations of Authority in Scotland and the British Isles* (Abingdon, Routledge, 2020).

Ditchburn, D., 'Trade with Northern Europe, 1297–1540', in Lynch M., Spearman M. and Stell G., (eds) *The Scottish Medieval Town* (Edinburgh: 1988), pp161–79.

BIBLIOGRAPHY

Dransart, P., Bennet, H., Bogdan, Thomas, C., Bryce, T. & Ryder, M., *Perth High Street Archaeological Excavation 1975–77 Fascicule 3 – the Textiles and Leather* (Perth, Tayside and Fife Archaeological Committee, 2012).

Duffy, S (ed.), *The World of the Galloglass: Kings, Warlords and Warriors in Ireland and Scotland 1200–1600* (Dublin, Four Courts Press, 2007, 2016).

Dunbar, J. T., *The History of Scottish Clothing*, (London, Batsford, 1981).

Dunbar, J. T., *History of Highland Dress,* (Edinburgh, Oliver & Boyd, 1962).

Fraser Mackintosh, *.Antiquarian Notes, 2nd Series.* (Inverness, A & W MacKenzie, 1897).

Fraser, Sir W., *The Sutherland Book* (Edinburgh, T& A Constable 1892.) 2 volumes.

Haslam, K., 'Leading the Charge?: Leadership in war in late medieval Scottish burghs,'" in *Martial Culture in Medieval Town*, 18/10/2021, https://martcult.hypotheses.org/1430.

Hayward M, *Rich Apparel: Clothing and Law in Henry VII's England* (London, Routledge, 2017)

Johnson, C., *The King's Servants: Men's Dress at the Accession of Henry VIII. A Tudor Tailor Case Study* (Guildford, Fat Goose Press, 2009).

Jones, R., *Bloody Banners: Martial Discipline on the Medieval Battlefield* (Woodbridge, Boydell & Brewer, 2010).

Jones, R. & Coss, P. R., *A Companion to Chivalry* (Woodbridge, The Boydell Press, 2019).

Kelvin, M., *The Scottish Pistol*, (London, Cyrus Arts, 1996).

Lee, J., T*he Medieval Clothie*r, (Woodbridge, Boydell & Brewer, 2018).

Irving, J. *The Book of Dumbartonshire: A History of the County, Burghs, Parishes, and Lands, Memoirs of Families, and Notices of Industries Carried on in the Lennox District.* (Edinburgh, 1879.)

MacCoinnich, A., 'His Spirit is Given Only to Warre': Conflict and Identity in the Scottish Gàidhealtachd, c.1580–c.1630', in Murdoch, S. and Mackillop, S. (eds), F*ighting for Identity: Scottish Military Experience c.1550–1900* (Leiden, Brill, 2002), pp.133–6.

Martin, C. A., 'Maritime Dominion – Sea-Power and the Lordship' in *The Lordship of the Isles*, Oram R. (Ed.) (Leiden, Brill, 2014) pp.176–199.

McClintock, H. F., *Old Irish and Highland Dress*, (Dundalk, Dundalgan Press, 1943).

MacDonald Fraser, G. *The Steel Bonnets: The Story of the Angle Scottish Border Reivers* (London, Pan Books, 1974).

Macdougall, N, *James III* (John Donald, Edinburgh, 1982).

MacGregor, Martin Gaelic barbarity and Scottish identity in the later Middle Ages. In: Broun, Dauvit and MacGregor, MacGregor, M. *The Campbells: lordship, literature and liminality. Textual Cultures: Texts, Contexts and Interpretation* (Indiana University Press, Bloomington, 2012) 7(1), pp.121–157.

Mackay, D. N. *Clan Warfare in the Scottish Highlands.* (Paisley: Alexander Gardner. 1922).

MacDonald, A, The Kingdom of Scotland at War: 1332–1488, in *A Military History of Scotland* eds Spiers, E, Crang, J, Strickland ((Edinburgh, Edinburgh University Press, 2012, 2014) pp.158–181.

MacLeod, R C, *The Book of Dunvegan, being documents from the muniment room of the MacLeods of MacLeod at Dunvegan Castle, Isle of Skye*, (Edinburgh, Third Spalding Club, 1938–9).

McLeod, W & Bateman, M (eds) *Duanaire Na Sracaire: Songbook of the Pillagers Anthology of Scotland's Gaelic Verse to 1600*, (Edinburgh, Origin, 2019).

MacGregor, M. Warfare in Gaelic Scotland in the Later Middle Ages', *A Military History of Scotland*, Spiers, E, Crang, J, Strickland (Eds), (Edinburgh, Edinburgh University Press, 2012, 2014) pp.209–221.

Mackenzie, R. *The Swords and the Sorrows*, (Glasgow, National Trust for Scotland, 1996)

Martin (eds) Mìorunmòr nan Gall, 'The great ill-will of the Lowlander'? Lowland perceptions of the Highlands, medieval and modern'. (Glasgow, Centre for Scottish and Celtic Studies, University of Glasgow, 2009), pp.7–48.

Merriman, M. *The Rough Wooings: Mary Queen of Scots 1542–1551*. (East Linton, Tuckwell Press, 2000).

Moffatt R., 'Crying over spilt Castlemilk: The Tale of Sir William and the Silver Sallet,' in *Martial* Culture in Medieval Town, (14/03/2021), https://martcult.hypotheses.org/1230

Moffatt, R. M., 'How Common Men Shall Be Armed: Equipment of the Common Soldier of England 1450 to 1500,' *in Martial Culture in Medieval Town*, (01/10/2021), https://martcult.hypotheses.org/1413.)

Moffat R. *A Sign of Victory? 'Scottish Swords' and Other Weapons in the Possession of the 'Auld Innemie'*, (Arms & Armour, 2000) pp122–143

Murdoch, S. *The Terror of the Seas? : Scottish Maritime Warfare, 1513–1713*. (Boston, Brill, 2010).

Peers, C., *The Highland Battles: Warfare on Scotland's Northern Frontier in the Early Middle Ages* (Barnsley, Pen and Sword, 2020)

Phillips, G, 'Scotland in the Age of Military Revolution, 1488–1560', Crang, J. A, Spiers, E. M & Strickland, M. J. (Eds), *A Military History of Scotland*, (Edinburgh, Edinburgh University Press, 2014) pp182–207.

Photos-Jones, 'Made in Scotland? Sword-Making in Scotland in the C15th & C16th in the Context of Recent Archaeological Evidence', in *Fields of Conflict: Progress & Prospect in Battlefield Archaeology*, ed. by P. W. M. Freeman and A. Pollard (Glasgow: Archaeopress, 2001), pp.61–72.

Pollard, T, The Archaeology of The Siege of Leith, 1560', in eds Pollard, T & Banks, I, B*astions and Barbed Wire : Studies in the Archaeology of Conflict*, (Leiden, Brill, 2009).

Rivett, Macleod M. *The Outer Hebrides: A Historical Guide* (Edinburgh, Birlinn, 2021).

Rixson, D, *The West Highland Galley*, (Edinburgh, Birlinn, 1998).

Small, G. The Scottish Court in the Fifteenth Century. 'A View from Burgundy', in Werner Paravicini (Hg.): *La cour de Bourgogne et l'Europe.*

Le rayonnement et les limites d'un mode leculturel; Actes du colloque international tenu à Paris les 9, 10 et 11 octobre 2007, avec le concours de Torsten Hiltmann et Frank Viltart, Ostfildern (Thorbecke 2013 Beihefte der Francia, 73) pp.457–474.

Schuessler, Bond, M. *Dressing the Scottish Court, 1543–1553: Clothing in the Accounts of the Lord High Treasurer of Scotland,* (Woodbridge, Boydell & Brewer, 2019).

Simms, K. '*From Kings to Warlords*' (Woodbridge, Boydell Press, 2000).

Steer, J. W. M & Bannerman, K. A. *Late Medieval Monumental Sculpture In The West Highlands* (Edinburgh, The Royal Commission on the Ancient & Historical Monuments of Scotland, 1977).

Stell, G, 'Late Medieval Defences in Scotland' in Caldwell, D (ed.), *Scottish Weapons and Fortifications* (Edinburgh, John Donald, 1981) pp 21–53.

Rhodes, E, *Edinburgh Castle: The Tournaments* (Edinburgh, Historic Environment Scotland, 2019)

Stevenson, D. *Highland Warrior: Alasdair MacColla and the Civil Wars* (Edinburgh, Saltire Society 1994), 21.

Stevenson, K.. 'Contesting Chivalry: James II and the control of chivalric culture in the 1450s', *Journal of Medieval History*, (London, Routledge, 2007) pp197–214,

Stevenson, K, 'Thai war callit knychtis and bere the name and the honour of that hye ordre': *Scottish Knighthood in the Fifteenth Century The Fifteenth Century VI: Identity and Insurgency in the late Middle Ages*, (Woodbridge, Boydell Press, 2006).

Tiramani, J., *A Spectacular Survivor from the Time of Henry VIII: The Study of a Mid Sixteenth Century Brigandine,* (Toronto: Royal Ontario Museum, 2010.)

The Royal Commission on the Ancient and Historical Monuments of Scotland, Argyll; Volume 7: Mid Argyll and Cowal: Medieval and Later Monuments (Edinburgh, HMSO, 1992).

Thomson, W., *The New History of Orkney,* (Edinburgh, Birlinn, 2012).

Whitelaw, C. A., Baxter, S. (eds) *Scottish Arms Makers: A Biographical Dictionary of Makers of Firearms, Edged Weapons and Armour Working in Scotland from the 14th Century to 1870* (London, Arms & Armour Press, 1977).

Secondary Sources: Articles

Armstrong, J. W., 'Local society and the Defence of the English frontier in Fifteenth Century Scotland: The War Measures of 1482', *Florilegium* 25 (Toronto, University of Toronto, 2008) pp.127–49.

Booker, S. 'Moustaches, mantles and saffron shirts: what motivated sumptuary law in medieval English Ireland?' *Speculum, 96 (3)*, 2021.

Brydall, R., 'Monumental effigies of Scotland from the thirteenth to the fifteenth century', in *Proceedings of the Society of Antiquaries of Scotland*, (Edinburgh,1894–5), pp.329–410.

Caldwell, D. H., 'Fragments of a Brigandine from Coldingham Priory, Berwickshire', *The Proceedings of the Society of Antiquaries of Scotland*, volume 106, (Edinburgh, The Society of Antiquaries of Scotland, 1974–75) pp.219–21.

Caldwell, D. H., 'How Well Prepared was James IV to Fight by Land and Sea in 1513?', *Journal of the Sydney Society for Scottish History*, volume 14, 2013, (Sydney 2013), pp.33–75.

Caldwell, D. H., 'The Defence of the Scottish Border', *Journal of the Sydney Society for Scottish History*, volume 12, 2010 (Sydney 2010), pp.59–81

Caldwell, D. H., 'Edinburgh Castle Under Siege, 1559–1573', *Journal of the Sydney Society for Scottish History*, volume 17, 2018 (Sydney 2018), pp.9–29.

Capwell, T. E., 'Observations on the Armour Depicted on Three mid–15th-Century Military Effigies in the Kirk of St. Nicholas, Aberdeen', *Journal of the Armour Research Society*, 1, 2005, pp.5–22.

Cathcart, A., 'The Forgotten '45: Donald Dubh's Rebellion in Archipelagic Context', *The Scottish Historical Review, vol. 91*, no 232, 2012, pp.239–264.

Cavendish, R,, 'James II of Scots killed at Roxburgh', *History Today*. 60 (8 August 2010).

Chambers, M., 'How Long is a Launce? Units of Measure for Cloth in Late Medieval Britain', *Medieval Clothing and Textiles, 13* (2017), pp.31–65.

Coltman Clephan, A. F.S.A., 'The Military Handgun of the Sixteenth Century', *Archaeological Journal*, 67:1, 1910, pp.109–150.

Dawson, J. 'The Fifth Earl of Argyle, Gaelic Lordship and Political Power in Sixteenth-Century Scotland', *The Scottish Historical Review*, (vol. 67, no. 183, 1988), pp.1–27.

Dickson, C. 'Food, Medicinal and Other Plants from the 15th Century Drains of Paisley Abbey, Scotland', *Vegetation History and Archaeobotany*, vol. 5, no. 1/2, (Springer.com, 1996) pp.25–31.

Dickinson, G. 'Some Notes on the Scottish Army in the First Half of the Sixteenth Century', *The Scottish Historical Review*, vol. 28, no. 106, (Edinburgh University Press, 1949) pp.133–45.

Ellis, S. G., 'The Collapse of the Gaelic World, 1450–1650', *Irish Historical Studies*, (Vol. 31, No. 124, Nov., 1999), pp.449–469.

Graham, A. 'The Battle of 'Sauchieburn'', *The Scottish Historical Review*, vol. 39, no. 128, (Edinburgh, Edinburgh University Press, 1960), pp.89–97.

Halpin, A. 'Irish Medieval Swords c. 1170–1600', *Proceedings of the Royal Irish Academy. Section C: Archaeology, Celtic Studies, History, Linguistics, Literature*, (vol. 86C, Royal Irish Academy, 1986), pp.183–230, http://www.jstor.org/stable/25506140.

Hanham, A., 'A medieval Scots Merchant's Handbook', *Scottish Historical Review* 50 (Edinburgh, Edinburgh University Press, 1971), pp107–20.

Hayes-McCoy, G. A., 'The Gallóglach Axe', *Journal of the Galway Archaeological and Historical Society*, (Vol. 17, No. 3/4 1937), pp.101–121

Hartshorne, A., 'The Sword Belts of the Middle Ages', *The Archaeological Journal* 48 (1891), pp.320–34.

BIBLIOGRAPHY

Hayward, M. 'Crimson, Scarlet, Murrey and Carnation: Red at the Court of Henry VIII', *Textile History 38:2* (November 2007)

Henshall, A., Crowfoot, G., Beckwith, J., 'Early textiles found in Scotland. Part II. Medieval Imports', *Proceedings of the Society of Antiquaries of Scotland* (Internet. 30Nov.1954) [cited 10 Aug.2021] pp22–9.

Henshall, A. & Maxwell, S., 'Clothing and other articles from a late 17th century grave at Gunnister, Shetland', *Proceedings of the Society of Antiquaries of Scotland*, (Iinternet,1951-2), [cited 12 December 2021] pp30–42.

Jennings, A, 'Latter-day Vikings: Gaels in the Northern Isles in the 16th Century', *Journal of the North Atlantic*, (Steuben, Eagle Hill, 2012) pp235–42.

Marshall, R, 'To be the Kingis Grace ane Dowblett': The Costume of James V, King of Scots', *Costume 28 No 1*, (Edinburgh, Edinburgh University Press, 1994), pp14–21.

McAleese, R. 'Aberdeen's Bedesmen: Poverty and Piety', *History Scotland*, Jan/Feb 2012, pp. 46–49.

McWhannell, Dr D.C., 'Campbell of Breadalbane and Campbell of Argyll Boatbuilding Accounts 1600 to 1700', *The Mariner's Mirror*, 89:4, 2003, pp405–424.

McWhannell, Dr D. C., 'The Galleys of Argyll', *The Mariner's Mirror*, 88:1, 2002, pp 14–32,

McWhannell, Dr D. C., 'Ship Service and Indigenous Sea Power in the West of Scotland', *West Highland Notes and Enquiries*, August 2000, Series 3, Vol.1, pp3–18.

Moffat, Dr R., 'A hard harnest man': The Armour of George Dunbar, 9th Earl of March', *Transactions of the East Lothian Antiquarian and Field Naturalists' Society* (North Berwick, Volume 30, 2015) pp21–38.

Moffat, R., 'The Manner of Arming Knights for the Tourney: A Re-interpretation of an important 14th Century Arming Treatise', *Arms & Armour Vol. 7, no. 1*, 2010, pp5–29.

Munro, J, 'The anti-red shift – to the 'Dark Side': Colour changes in Flemish luxury woollens, 1300 – 1550', *Medieval Clothing and Textiles , Vol. 3, No. 1* 2007, pp.55–98.

Murphy, N. 'The Duke of Albany's Invasion of England in 1523 and Military Mobilisation in Sixteenth-century Scotland', *The Scottish Historical Review 2020* 99.1, 1–25.

Penman M. A., 'Christian days and Knights: the religious devotions and court of David II of Scotland, 1329–71', *Historical Research Vol. 75, no. 189, 2002*, pp.249–272.

Phillips, G., 'In the Shadow of Flodden: Tactics, Technology and Scottish Military Effectiveness, 1513–1550', *The Scottish Historical Review, vol. 77, no. 204, 1998*, pp.162–182.

Phillips, G. 'Irish 'Ceatharnaigh' in English Service, 1544–1550, and the Development of Gaelic Warfare', *Journal of the Society for Army Historical Research, vol. 78, no. 315*, London, Society for Army Historical Research.

Phillips, G, 'The Employment of War Dogs in the Medieval and Early Modern West', *British Journal for Military History, 7.1* (2021), pp.2–20.

Shaw, F., 'Sumptuary Legislation in Scotland', *Judicial Review 24.* 1979, pp81–115 (Edinburgh, Edinburgh University Press).

Smith, P. 'On the Fringe and in the Middle: The MacDonalds of Antrim and the Isles 1266–1586', *History Ireland, vol. 2, no. 1*, 1994, pp.15–20.

Stevenson, K., 'The Unicorn, St Andrew and the Thistle: Was There an Order of Chivalry in Late Medieval Scotland?', *The Scottish Historical Review*, vol. 83, no. 215, (Edinburgh, Edinburgh University Press,2004), pp.3–22, http://www.jstor.org/stable/25529752. Accessed 27 Apr. 2022.

Swinton, George S. C. 'John of Swinton: A Border Fighter of the Middle Ages', *The Scottish Historical Review*, vol. 16, no. 64, pp.261–79 (Edinburgh University Press, 1919).

Tarrant, N., 'The 17th-century doublet from Keiss, near Wick, Caithness', *Proceedings of the Society of Antiquaries of Scotland, 131*, pp 319–326. Retrieved from http://journals.socantscot.org/index.php/psas/article/view/9560

Watt, Douglas, "The Laberinth of Thir Difficulties': The Influence of Debt on the Highland Elite c. 1550 – 1700,' *The Scottish Historical Review*, vol. 85, no. 219, (Edinburgh University Press, 2006), pp.28–51.

White. D. G., 'Henry VIII's Irish Kerne in France and Scotland', *Irish Sword*, iii 1957–8, pp.213–25.

Wilcox, D., Payne, S., Pardoe, T. & Mikhaila, N., 'A Seventeenth Century Doublet from Scotland', *Costume, vol. 2011, no. 45*, pp.39–62.

Willemsen, A., 'Taking Up the Glove: Finds, Uses and Meanings of Gloves, Mittens and Gauntlets in Western Europe, c. AD 1300–1700', *Post-Medieval Archaeology 49, no. 1 2015*, pp.1–36.

Willis, T., 'The Scottish Two Handed Sword', *ASAC Bulletin – Volume 120 September 2019*, pp.35–69.

Secondary Sources: Unpublished

Crawford, R. M., 'Warfare in the West Highlands and Isles of Scotland, c. 1544–1615'. (Glasgow, unpublished PhD thesis, 2016).

Wiseman, A. E. M. 'Chasing the Deer, Hunting Iconography and tradition in the Scottish Highlands, (Edinburgh, unpublished PhD thesis, 2007).

Secondary Sources: Websites

French, M. https://flemish.wp.st-andrews.ac.uk/2015/11/06/guns-and-gunpowder-in-late-medieval-scotland-influences-from-flanders/ Accessed September 2021

The database of the University of Manchester Lexis of Cloth and Clothing Project http://lexisproject.arts.manchester.ac.uk.